GAMES WITHOUT FRONTIERS

GAMES WITHOUT FRONTIERS

Fun, Growth & Development

Games For Group Workers

PIP WILSON

MarshallPickering
An Imprint of HarperCollins*Publishers*

Marshall Pickering is an Imprint of
HarperCollins*Religious*
Part of HarperCollins*Publishers*
77–85 Fulham Palace Road,
Hammersmith, London W6 8JB

First published in Great Britain
in 1988 by Marshall Morgan & Scott
(now Marshall Pickering)
5 7 9 10 8 6 4

A catalogue record for this book is
available from the British Library

ISBN 0 551 01554 3

Set in Times

Printed in Great Britain by
HarperCollinsManufacturing Glasgow

Acknowledgements

THANK YOU'S are due to the many helpers over many years on the Frontiers. Secretaries Liz, Mo and Gill, teams of workers including MoiraMo and The Rolling Magazine Team who work with me – especially at Greenbelt Arts Festival. Thanks too to the many volunteers for their commitment, enthusiasm, energy and risk that leaves its mark in more beautiful human persons.

To other contributors to this book and my life – Thank you. Especially: Ian Long for his artistic creation. Jenny Orpwood for her disability awareness. Howard Searle for his crystal clear poems.

Lastly, our beautiful little Wilson 'Hug Family', Joan, Joy, and Ann. Thank you.

Pip Wilson BHP.

Contents

Dedication

This book is dedicated to the late JIM PUNTON, who died in 1986 having passed on so much from his life as a Youthworker, Trainer, Bible Scholar, Supervisor and National Training Officer for Frontier Youth Trust.
A man of Shalom.

Pip Wilson, October 1987

Foreword

Games we all remember from our childhood, but we remain, sometimes secretly, total fans of them.

Pip Wilson stretches the frontiers with his games – some that could **only** be played with the wildest of youthful energy – others that would fit easily into most social occasions. Family get-togethers – youth clubs – schools – camps – churches etc.

Other games stretch the frontiers of, not only vigour and imagination, but they also stretch the parts of us that other games cannot reach. They touch the body mind and spirit.

I've tasted the energy and challenge of some of these games at the Greenbelt Festival.

It is your turn to extend your repertoire of Games – without Frontiers.

Roy Castle

A Special Note to You

You are a Beautiful Human Person as you read this.

Read this and absorb it — don't read these words flippantly. Are you reading? They are written for *YOU* especially *YOU*.

You are a valuable person
You are a special person
You are a unique person
You are beautiful
You are precious
You are unrepeatable
You are mysterious
You are a beautiful human person
No one will ever exist like you
No one will ever experience a life that you have experienced
You are a collection of specialness that has never been put together before
Your life deserves a film premiere at a West End cinema
You are so special and valuable that Jesus has died for you
He loves you so much that he has given his life for you
His love is completely and totally 100% for you
His love for *you* is unconditional

If you became a better person *now*, if you became a committed Christian *today* — either or both, God couldn't love you any more tomorrow.
His love for you is total *NOW* and he cannot love you any more. Of course he deserves a response and it makes him happy if we respond *BUT* his love is not dependent on it. You are 100%, totally and completely loved.

Pip Wilson

Copyright

Games The games in this book can be photocopied and used in the small group context — but not reprinted without author's/publisher's permission. For any material used please acknowledge the source.

Games sources. A number of these games have been around for a long time — and known by many. Others have been invented by me in a wild moment. Others have been adapted, changed and developed over the many years of being a gamester. Please forgive me if you think I've nicked your game — you have most likely nicked one of mine!

Section One
An Introduction to Games

Learning through Games

If we don't communicate, receive or transmit, we may as well be dead. If we don't try to develop our communication skills we may as well say we are *dying* not *living*. We are told that 80% of all communication is non-verbal communication. The 'verbal' is very much second place to how we communicate with our eyes, smiles, touch, manner, expression, hands, arms, feet, our attitude, our motivation, our spirit, our listening, our energy and in fact our whole body and presence. What Christians call the 'incarnation' is Jesus becoming flesh and dwelling amongst us.

It is so exciting that God loved the World so much that he didn't send Jesus to stand on a cloud and shout down words and rules of life, he sent his most beautiful Human Person — his son Jesus to communicate with body, mind and spirit!

The best form of communication it seems to me only happens when it happens in *the flesh*. Jesus set the example of communicating with people. It was thirty years before he started 'talking'! What I mean is, he lived for thirty years before he started his public ministry. He was crucified at the age of thirty-three. Whatever I write about games and other methods of communication it must always be against the backdrop of incarnational love — Jesus style.

Games are one modern method of communication. You may say 'not *so* modern'. You would be correct. Many different cultures around the world have games which are very meaningful. We have learned in the past by playing games, and I would suggest that we can continue to *learn through games*.

Games Without Frontiers reflects my culture and my journey through life. The teams and young people I have worked alongside have given me so much, and there is so much more to learn.

But games are childish you may say! Many adults love games because we have all got a 'child' within us. Games it seems to me, can be *safe* learning. We can enjoy each other, relax and learn at the same time! A strength of games is their humour — there is nothing like laughing for relaxing with people of all races/ages. You can *watch* football on a Saturday afternoon, you can *watch* snooker on TV, you *watch* your favourite soap but Games without Frontiers *you play*!

There are games, however, that *I don't like*. When I am in groups playing word games like Scrabble or spelling games I always feel inferior. I feel inadequate, I squirm and feel like running away. These Games without Frontiers, if played properly, don't create bad feelings or inadequacy or competition but relaxation and development. The participants need to be able to trust the leader — quickly.

As you read you will be deciding whether or not to trust me. I have this philosophy — take what you need. What I write here is *my truth* not *the* truth. Take from it what you need. The bits that interest you take. Allow what you *do not* need to run through your fingers like sand. What *is* of use to you, hold in both hands and mould, adapt and add from your own culture, personality and your unique experience.

This book has been written from a backdrop as a Youth Worker with the personal aim in life to see the beautiful people whom God has made and bled for, become even more beautiful. Some Youth Workers would say 'you mean Social Education or Personal Development for young people!' I say that the Good News of Jesus is about wholeness. About young and old 'becoming mature . . . attaining to the whole measure . . . of the fullness of Christ . . .' (Ephesians 4:13). I believe that we are all made in the image of God, special, beautiful, with unique qualities and with the full potential of the Creator himself. This belief motivates me to hold in parallel (i) self discovery, Creator discovery, people discovery and a general growing awareness and (ii) stimulating, confronting and learning from others as we travel along the same tracks.

> I want to disturb the comfortable and comfort the disturbed!
>
> *Howard Snyder* (Liberating the Church, Marshalls, 1983)

To play a mixture of games similar to 'Games without Frontiers' will never re-enforce the status quo but create a whole package of interactive concrete communication.

What is concrete communication?

Churches and other organisations churn out literature in *concepts*. Here is a rush of them — sin, salvation, redemption, forgiveness, justification; that will do because I'm falling asleep myself ALREADY!! z z z z z z . . .

The non-academic mind isn't a selection of linear files, it is much more like a pop-video library. When a sermon or talk is heard often it is the story bit, *the illustration*, that turns the ears to the ON position and is easily remembered. Often the *application* of the story is turned off quickly because it is not made quickly enough but droned about in the most boring way. Jesus, my Master, often told stories without *any* application and trusted the people themselves to remember it and apply it. An under used method! It seems to me that real dynamic communication is played upon a video screen inside the non-academic head because it is concrete communication. (Stories with a beginning and an end communicate. Visual aids can be recorded and played back on the video in the mind. *That is concrete communication*.)

The London-based *EastEnders* TV programme, like it or cringe it, is concrete communication. It is a story that people can relate to. It isn't a list of related concepts which often we see on talking-heads programmes. The whole *EastEnders*/soaps thing is an issue I could write about for pages; but here are just a *few* points.

It is good, it seems to me, because it is gripping, relaxing and stimulating. Real life issues are brought into the family home more personally and powerfully than in the tabloids. It can be a real awareness raising programme on subjects like suicide, sexual assault, depression, the menopause, racism etc. Racism in its direct form, is distant from some communities but *EastEnders* can make it very real at the feelings level.

This reminds me of a quote by Tom Houston in a document called 'The Communication of the Good News in a Television Age' (Bible Society)

> In a TV age, one of the things people want is a sense of belonging. That is why especially today it takes a community to communicate the good news and offer a place to feel at home. (p. 14)

That East End Square, that Street and even that infamous TV oil city communicate a fantasy community. What worries me is that I see so many people who only experience 'community' via a TV screen. Playing games can be a 'community making' experience rather than the 'community breaking' experiences dished up in the education services and particularly in the church services. In my view, the TV-type of community de-skills so many people from discovering community for themselves.

Second-best communication is often satisfactory *only* because a better style of life is outside their experience. What the soaps do show is that people need 'community' in their lives and that's what Tom Houston is writing about! We Christians need to be *in* community, *living* community, *experiencing* community (not in a narrow sense), then others will join and 'feel at home'.

I vote for concrete communication. Games are concrete in that they are experiences not concepts. I am not saying 'Games to take over the world!' But games can contribute to Jesus' Kingdom on earth. I am a Kingdom person. What does a Kingdom person do? 'Church people think about how to get people into Church. Kingdom people think about how to get the church into the world', says Howard Snyder.

I write *as* a Christian Church person but determined to remain uncomfortable within it. As U2 sing 'I believe in the Kingdom come when all the colours bleed into one — *but I still* haven't found what I'm looking for'.

The Band/Snyder say it for me . . .

When Christians put the Church ahead of the Kingdom, they settle for the status quo and their own kind of people.

The Basics of Communication

Communication is basically an act of sending and receiving. Sending in such a clear way that the Receiver can recreate the exact communication within themselves.

Sending — feelings, ideas and signals.
Receiving — ideas, feelings and signals.

A simple example of communication is *The Morse Code*. Sender and Receiver share a code. S.O.S., for example = Save Our Souls = distress = emergency. Even with this simple example of communication there remains confusion.

If it is ship to ship, for instance, is the ship sinking? Is there a fire? Have lives been lost or in danger? So much must be left to the imagination and the purpose of good communication is to leave the minimum to the imagination. Concrete communication is clear, precise communication. Clear and precise to both the Sender and the Receiver.

I like to visualise precise communication like strands of stainless steel wire running from the Sender to the Receiver. The problem is that we don't often have concrete communication, and to add to that we have our in-built inferiority complex. The wires then become covered in fluff. This fluff becomes tacky and sticky like candy floss which is the imagination surrounding our communication. Many of the games here are aimed at clearing that fluff. Self-revelation cancels the negative side of imagination.

If we wish to communicate effectively, it will help to be aware that there are *five kinds of communication*.

1 *Intrapersonal*	=	Communication with self, within self via our self-questioning both conscious and sub-conscious.
2 *Interpersonal*	=	Communication between two people. Both sending and receiving.
3 *Small Group*	=	Communication within a group small enough to allow all members to interact. All are senders and receivers.
4 *Public*	=	Communication from one

		person to many, which reduces considerably the feedback from the receivers.
5 *Media*	=	Communication via TV, Radio, magazines, newspapers, books, leaflets etc. This method relies on the sender being aware of the receiver's needs and interests as there is no interaction.

What are the essentials when it comes to communicating?

a. It seems to me we need to know and accept ourselves.

(i) You need to know that you are valuable, special, unique, incredibly precious, mysterious and unrepeatable. You are so special and unique that already your life deserves a biography. No-one has ever, or will ever have a life like yours. *You* **are** *special and valuable*. So valuable that Jesus has died for you. His love for you is total and unconditional and 100%. His love for you is so complete that if you became perfect today — he couldn't love you any more tomorrow. He cannot love you more than he does right now. (Of course God desires that we respond to him — and it pleases him if we do.)

If God accepts us and loves us — why not accept and love ourselves too?

(ii) We also need to *know* ourselves and that includes strengths and weaknesses. We all have them and it seems to me we need to 'own' them. No use saying 'If only', 'I wish I . . .', 'If only I'd had a better education . . . a job . . . a smaller nose . . . a bigger bust . . .'

Sometimes I feel frustrated because I can't offer the people around me what they need! Or sometimes they get me down and I can't handle that! I have a saying — sometimes to myself — sometimes to others:

'*THE WHOLENESS YOU REQUIRE I DO NOT HAVE*'.

b. We need to have a big commitment to communication not just to make our point of view. If you believe in love and all people being valuable because they have been created in God's image, then love! Love isn't a plaque that you hang on a wall — it's something you *do to people*!

No matter if we are sending or receiving, our motivation needs to be love. Always love. People with or without faith agree with the Bible (1 Cor. 13) and its love verses. It's just that we tend to be selective in our application.

c. We need to communicate from a position of vulnerability. Feelings communicate if you can send them! The most powerful communication I have experienced has been with the toughest of young people when I have shared my vulnerability. I remember the time I was upset when my elderly mum was preparing to go into hospital to have both her legs amputated. I chatted about it to a number of young men aged between 18–26 years. All of them would be described as delinquent and most had committed serious crimes of violence. I shared the pain from my guts and they received it. They also kept in touch by checking on the news during the following weeks as my mother recovered from the operation. My authentic vulnerability communicated directly and created concrete communication of eternal significance.

In our weakness is our strength.

d. It is essential to accept and love kids *where they are*! A whole jumble of informal interactions is necessary before a people-person can suss out where the receiver is at. We need to understand the receiver's culture, education, language range, personality, interests, strengths and weaknesses.

David Sheppard was asked what he was going to do when he became Bishop of Liverpool. This man of great experience of inner city London, both at the Mayflower Family Centre and as Bishop of Woolwich said that he was going to listen and learn. Incredible! The whole issue of contextualising the gospel is making it relevant to the culture that we desire to communicate within.

Accept the kids where they are not where you would like them to be.

God so loved the world that he didn't send young Christians on a *one week mission* to evangelise the inner city.

Concrete communication

When it comes to communication, it seems to me, we must talk about *groups*. There is great need for one-to-one work with teenagers and development of the skills needed. Contact-making skills cannot be underestimated; neither can confrontational methods, counselling, social skills training, political and social education skills and so on.

Groupwork, it seems to me is the most essential for any Youth Worker/people-person. Talk about kids/teenagers/young and old people, and you talk about peer groups. Often the kids who are most disturbed are those who *don't* or can't associate with a friendship group. In my years working in the inner city it was the single young man or young woman who didn't belong to a criminalised gang or group that concerned me. The social norm was to be an offender, and *not* to be a 'tea leaf' (a thief) was to be an 'odd ball' or a 'psycho'. It was a whole reversal of norms.

Even young people who made a Christian commitment used to worry me if they didn't belong to a delinquent gang! For more on this — see my book *Gutter Feelings*, (Marshall Pickering, 1985).

The majority of humans relate to groups and in groups. There is so much to learn about the processes of groups that it excites me as I continue to discover. I would recommend the group work books by John Mallison (Scripture Union, 1978) and by Tom Douglas (Tavistock Publications, 1978). Worth a special mention is Jean Grigor's book *Grow to Love* (St. Andrews Press, 1977). It is a great little book — much better than the taste you get in this *Games without Frontiers*.

Jesus worked with individuals, with large crowds and with families, using many different forms of communication. It seems to me that he used, most of all, the small group method of communication. 'Come with me and I will make you fishers of men.'

To communicate concretely with passion, motivation and commitment, we need to stretch our own comfort boundaries.

If we remain in status quo and comfortable we will not grow and develop. We all have boundaries in our lives where we can move around and yet stay comfortable. We stay within these boundaries because *outside them* we experience feelings of discomfort and that makes us feel insecure.

All our lives we have been establishing these boundaries to help us to handle our insecurity. We all have a built-in inferiority complex but yet the way to growth and development *for us* is outside those boundaries. To 'start where they are at' is within *their* comfort boundaries.

Being a motivated communicator is costly.
Being a motivated Christian communicator is more costly.
Christians are called to love the unlovely.
Christians are called to disturb the comfortable and comfort the disturbed.

Seek the Shalom of the City where I have sent you . . . and pray to the Lord on its behalf; for in its Shalom you will find your own Shalom.

(Jeremiah 29:6–7)

General Tips for Game Leaders

Glance down quickly and read the bits that stand out.

When leading a games evening, games session or just one game before each activity — THINK AND PLAN.

1. First of all **collect the facts**. I always sit down with an A4 pad and doodle. Up 'til then a games session plays on my mind. Once I've

committed it to paper I seem to relax *so* much more. See Appendix One.

2. What do you know about the *Environment*? Church Hall? School Hall? Youth Club? Church? Home? Community Centre? Tenants Association Hall? Open Field? Marquee? If you don't know the answers to all these questions above or below — stinkin' ask!!

3. What is the **lighting** like? Can it be adjusted by you or someone else? The lighting can be important. A cold white light can create tension and formality. Dull lighting can hinder audience participation because they can't see the fun. Bright but colourful lighting could be just right!

4. What about **room size**? Is it too big? Rooms can usually be partitioned with little trouble by using notice boards, coatracks, litterbins, seating etc. A room too big can create an uncomfortable atmosphere. A room too small can hinder the type of games you are planning to use.

5. **Seating** is important. Don't have a room with rows of chairs facing you. It's more informal to have kids sitting on the floor, on cushions or some on chairs, window ledges etc. It's important that people can see each other because most of the fun comes from group life.

6. **Numbers** of people can influence the atmosphere greatly! Some games *need* large numbers to create the spectacle and encourage participants to smash eggs on someone's head for instance! A small group can be more intimate — perhaps develop more quickly into playing more games with body contact.

7. Do members of the group know each other? Will it be **one group or two**? If it is one youth group for instance there will be 'in jokes' and 'in acts' of behaviour and young people playing certain roles. If more than one group — be aware that one group could dominate because of its size or home territory.

8. When there are **adults and leaders** amongst a young people's group nothing can be worse than them being non-participants. Encourage them and love them into the games. The informal contact and other bits of communication that develop can be incredible for making contact and developing relationships. A tomato smashed against the Vicar's forehead can have incredibly good spin-offs in terms of future relationships!

9. What is the **age** of the participants? You may have to lead a group with a whole spectrum of ages, and that can be a beautiful experience of bringing generations together. You could however create rejection feelings for some if you start off with seemingly

inappropriate games. Each age group will need acknowledging. Affirm the ones who are most vulnerable and ill at ease.

10. **Urban kids** can be totally different in their responses. Will they be young 'dash-about types'? Will they be laid back 'you're not getting *me* to do anything — mate!' types? Will they be 'let's smash up the equipment and . . .' types?

11. Be **flexible** with all games and groups. The games enclosed are not 'gospel'. Adapt, mix, change them according to your need.

12. What about the programme **before and after**? Be aware of what *has* gone on because it could have created a certain climate. You will have a starting point there. Don't be like the farmer giving instructions to a lost rambler 'O, I wouldn't start from here'! Starting 'where they are' must be on your agenda. Also what follows is important. Do you go out with a bang, with a big build-up of excitement at the end or do you end on a point of reflection, emotion, sensitivity to others, consideration for neighbours or others perhaps less fortunate than ourselves? Think and plan the last game.

13. **Expectations** are important. Every single person will have slightly different expectations of *you*, *the session* and the purpose. Everyone will also have their own agenda from home, work or school. Some will be excited — some extremely sad. There will be dynamics between people in the group. Some will sit at the other end of the room to avoid the slightest contact with another. One or more will feel isolated from the group and will show it in their seating position. Some will expect the worst, and others much more than you, or the group, can possibly give. A great number will be nervous or apprehensive at the start of a weekend house party for instance. If you are leading a first session for a weekend, it seems to me it is the most important session. Think on paper about this one. Note the range of expectations so that *your* expectations will be as soundly based as possible.

14. **Sensitivity** is very important. Among groups of people, more often than not, there are people who are carrying hurt, are lonely, feel angry, have been abused, feel inferior, feel very tender about their sexuality, feel bitter about authority and even leaders of games sessions! The best tip I can offer on this one is, to affirm constantly. Affirming is more than encouragement, it is an attitude of valuing people, seeing the positives in people and demonstrating you care by actions and words. Games, it seems to me, need to emphasise the co-operative 'fun' aspect and not the competition winner/loser syndrome. If you have eyes to see and ears to hear, as Jesus said, then develop your awareness of what is happening around you. Don't just look at a pile of bodies.

Really notice individuals. All of them — but especially those on the margins, tense faces, the first through the door and the last through the door. (Have you realised the significance of two or more young people walking into a room? Who *is* first? Who is second? Who is last? Does it always happen?*

* See Chapter Eight of my *Gutter Feelings* for more on this subject (Marshalls, 1985)

15. Don't **moan and groan** and force people to join in! 'You don't have to join in folks', I often say 'but you'll love it — let yourself go'. With lots of non-threatening enthusiasm. Don't forget they need to join in for their benefit *not* to please you!
16. On planning a games session it is important to have a repertoire of games and equipment. To have a large range of options helps as you read the atmosphere and then decide on the next game. I have 'cue' cards in my back pocket with one/two word titles of games under categories like the ones listed in this book. With a quick shuffle I can glance down the list and instantly pull out the next game to suit the next stage of development.
17. **Team work** is very important in gaming. In a fast moving games session it seems to me that one person needs to be taking the lead, but team work is essential. Music can create the atmosphere you desire and music during the games adds to the excitement. Someone needs to be responsible for this, plus scene shifting, wiping up the mess, preparing the materials, joining in and participating at an ever increasing level. Team work should equip every member not de-skill them.
18. What are the **aims** of the organiser? What are *your* aims? Do you just wish to 'have fun' or create a personal impact? Do you want the majority to enjoy it or do you wish it to be a positive experience for every single person present? Do you think young people 'should' do this and 'ought' to do that, or be such and such? Do you want to meet people where they are *at* and encourage them to become more whole, balanced individuals? Do you want to facilitate them to reach their God-given potential? Just look at people and love them *as they are*. Just love people and desire that they grow into liberated individuals. Love is unconditional it seems to me. Love desires the best for individuals, groups, communities, nations and beyond even that. To desire more than growth is oppressive.
19. Finally read through the whole book and mark the games you like or are relevant to your group. I *repeat myself* but be flexible and make them work for you. Also invent your own games using

normal everyday materials. Keep a file of them (and send me a copy!!). Then 'go for it'. Games work by enthusiasm so put your guts into games.

Warnings

1. Always have a *First Aid Kit* available.
2. Never press, force or embarrass a person to play a game. Encouragement is the best.
3. Be aware of the odd one out.
4. Be aware of people who are disabled.
5. Don't play 'emotionally stirring' games unless you can give the experience and the time to work through the effects.

Feelings Games

When games involve role play or any form of experiencing feelings (e.g. page 000 observer games), there must always be time given to what the training professionals call de-roling.

At one training weekend that I was involved with a young woman played a role for less than one minute, which included violence and aggression. She carried those intense feelings for the rest of the weekend because she wasn't de-roled. That is bad news in a context which is intending to be a 'good news' learning experience.

De-roling

Get all involved in the feelings experience to

1. Spend time talking about those feelings in a small group of people who they are familiar with and trust.
2. Have them talk freely about their feelings in the role play. Then look at the role from outside and analyse what had happened when 'in role'.

   See also *Special Note* on page 168.

Games for People with Disabilities by Jenny Orpwood

Included with each game is a guide as to whether or not a game is suitable for a person with a physical disability; a person who is deaf or has a hearing loss; and people who are blind or have a visual disability. The guide is only a rough indicator and should not necessarily be adhered to. As each person varies and is individual, so is disability, whether physical, perceptual or intellectual. It is, therefore, necessary to be sensitive to a person's abilities, rather than concentrating on disabilities.

I hope the following notes will help you to make a choice of games when working in a group of people with mixed abilities and disabilities.

Physical disability

An individual with a physical disability may be in a wheelchair, may walk on crutches or with aids, may walk unaided, or have a disability that affects their arms. The disability may affect the whole body. This may mean an individual is unable to speak clearly, and may have poor mouth and throat control. Be wary of this in games involving holding things in the mouth. Limbs may be paralysed and have no feeling. Injury may occur without an individual knowing. This doesn't mean that she/he can't take part, but that a participant needs to know what is expected in the game and, therefore, know the risks involved.

It may be difficult for some people to dress and undress — be sensitive to this in games where it's required. ASK if help is required and what help is required. Some people with physical disability have learning problems — be sensitive in games requiring reading etc.

Visual disability

Very few people are totally blind. However, the degree to which some one can see will vary greatly. It may be useful, for example, to have materials such as the poems and blob pictures at the end of the book enlarged, which will aid many. Again, ask what help is required.

If lots of games are being played, ensure that not all of them involve just 'seeing' what's happening for the audience. It may be possible to 'see' people running backwards and forwards but not 'see' a face being made up. A good MC, giving a running commentary, will add to the atmosphere for everyone. Be sensitive when using reading or spelling games.

Hearing Disabilities

Again the degree of hearing loss will vary greatly. Those people who have extreme hearing loss may have poor speech also. Make sure that a person who is deaf is in the best position for seeing the person talking.

In discussion groups ask individuals to indicate when they are about to speak, check that the lighting is good and that people don't cover their mouths, chew gum etc. whilst speaking. There's no need to shout — but speak clearly and at a moderate rate. Speaking very slowly distorts the mouth shape of the word. Writing things down may help. Many people who are deaf 'sign' — perhaps the group or leader could go on a course if appropriate. Again ask what's best for that person.

For people with a mental handicap it is difficult to give guidelines. Those given above for physical or perceptual handicaps may apply especially if an individual has a multiple disability. Remember to be sensitive when using word games — games which give the lead (like 'follow my leader') may be appropriate.

The most important point is to ensure that when a game is meant to include every one — that it does.

I've often been in a group in which the initial activity excludes some one with a disability. If a game is played to build the feeling of 'group' — make sure it does.

Don't be frightened of adapting games to suit the abilities of all people whether disabled or not.

Guides to games

	those with a visual disability
	those with a physical disability
	those with a hearing disability
√	most likely appropriate
X	most likely not appropriate
?	will suit some people

JENNY ORPWOOD – aged thirty-one, born in the East End of London, contracted polio at the age of three and consequently uses a wheelchair. Interest in sport stemmed from having hydro-therapy as a toddler. She gradually moved into international competition by the age of sixteen. Represented Great Britain for twelve years as a paraplegic swimmer, including four Olympic Games.

Trained as a teacher and gained a degree in education; main subjects: Social Biology and Education; subsidiary subjects: Science and PE.

After graduating worked for Social Services in Newham for eighteen months, gaining experience from people with either physical, or perceptual (deafness or blindness) disabilities. Then taught for six years in Elizabeth Fry School, Newham – a school for children with physical disabilities and learning handicaps, where her main responsibility was developing swimming and PE as well as those of a general class teacher.

Two years ago moved to Romford YMCA where she is Secretary for Sports & Recreation.

Jenny is also involved with The British Sports Association for Disabled People, both at a regional and national level.

Section Two
Total Participation Games

Total Participation

Introduction

1. Some of the best games are those that can be used to get *everyone* involved. I have used these games with two thousand teenagers all at once or in somewhat smaller groups, for example in someone's home.
2. Some will need a little preparation. Most need no equipment at all.
3. Remember that the leader must be sensitive (see General Tips).
4. The advantages of games for everyone are:

- The first game in a session, week-end, house party etc. often *breaks the ice* and therefore changes the atmosphere. (Choose one that will be appropriate!!)
- Everyone gets involved by smiling, laughing, touching and generally becoming less self conscious. Interaction inside a group is dynamic — *always* different, always *new*.
- Everyone belongs.
- The game becomes a shared experience. Everyone knows that everyone has played it and presumes that everyone feels the feelings.
- The game creates a central focus which helps create a cohesiveness in a group whatever the size.
- Total participation cultivates the co-operative nature of an event. No losers. Everyone wins. No spectators. No nervous people waiting around for their turn.
- Exclusion games are always second best; encourage people to participate. Never threaten, embarrass or use any kind of pressure. Encourage the participants to encourage others.

The aims of total participation games

1. Good fun through interaction.
2. Ice breaking before other activities.
3. Developing deeper relationship by mainly non-verbal means.
4. Participation creates body life that 'builds up' which is contrary to many activities in society. By participating closely with the lives of others we can be used by the Spirit of God to embody his love — in action.

5. Action games stimulate discovery learning. We teach in several ways. Thinking, feeling etc. Games are for *doing*.

I see I forget
I do I remember

1 Spellbummed
2 Skin the Snake
3 Knee Sit
4 Blind Lift
5 Belly Laughs
6 Birthday Row
7 Rainmaker
8 Animal Labels
9 Getting Your Hand In
10 Get Knotted
11 Clean T-Shirt
12 Ring-a-Ring-a-Roses
13 Circle of Trust
14 Head Balancing Act
15 Stiff as a Board
16 It's a Tick
17 Electric Shock
18 Spell It
19 Bump Bums
20 Hug Circle
21 Game For a Laugh
22 Straws
23 Lace up
24 Making Rain

SPELLBUMMED

1

👁	♿	✎
?	X	√

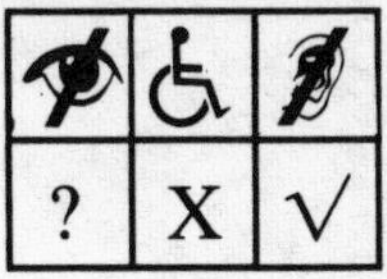

Spellbummed

Numbers

Everybody (minimum 3 – 10)

Equipment

None

Details

Get a volunteer comic to demonstrate. With his back to audience the idea is to spell name with bum and hip movements.

Get everyone into small groups and have them 'spell' their date of birth, or favourite pop singer etc.

Get the 'best' to demonstrate on stage.

Be flexible by using people's natural talent. The Vicar could be good at this!!

You try spelling Blodwyn

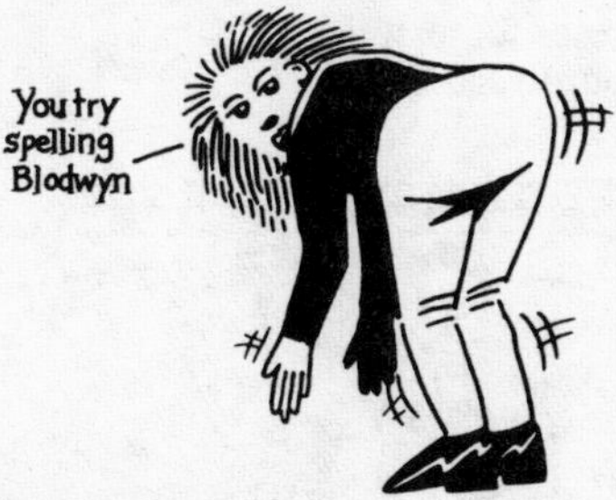

2

👁	♿	🎣
?	X	√

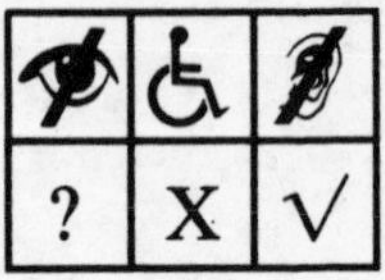

Skin the Snake

Numbers

Everybody (minimum 5); 8–10 in groups would be ideal.

Equipment

None

Details

Get everybody into groups in lines facing in the same direction. Tight formation. The left hand is pushed between your own legs and grasps the right hand of person behind. On the word 'go' the last person moves forward in a crouched or lying position while the rest of team shuffle back crouching in turn.

Special notes

Expect chaos, lots of physical contact, laughter, and lots of collapses! If it's completed, congratulate the team effort.
Affirm those who were unsuccessful.
Try for the world (group) record.

They have a funny way of shaking hands here

3

√	X	√

Knee Sit

Numbers

Everybody (minimum 8–10)

Equipment

None

Details

Get everyone into groups of approximately 10. Form into circles with the same shoulder facing into the centre and tightly packed close to one another. On the word 'go', the group should slowly sit down on the knees of the person behind them. When successful the next phase is to walk, or shuffle around with hands in the air to the beat of music.

Special notes

The circle must be 'round' and the tighter packed the better. Expect heaps of people.
Try two groups together! Then try a big one, with *everyone* in one circle.

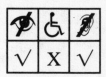

4

?	X	√

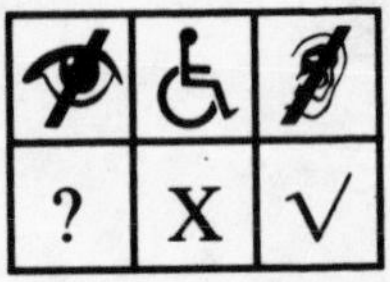

Blind Lift

Numbers

Everybody (minimum 7–8)

Equipment

None

Details

Ask everyone to form into groups of 7 to 10.

One group member lies on his back on the floor, with his eyes closed. The others stand at the sides from head to toes. Then very slowly lift — *gently* — and rock the person at waist height.
Slowly raise the person completely to the full extent of their arms and *gently* lower.

Special notes

This is not a rough game, but it should be played at the appropriate time.
It is important to emphasise the gentleness of it.
Encourage groups to offer pleasing experience of trust.
Give time to discuss the 'feelings' afterwards.

Mmm... this could easily replace massage...

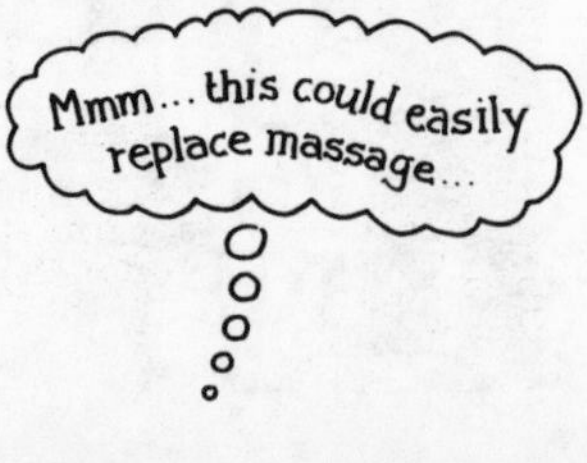

BELLY LAUGHS

5

👁	♿	🏃
√	X	?

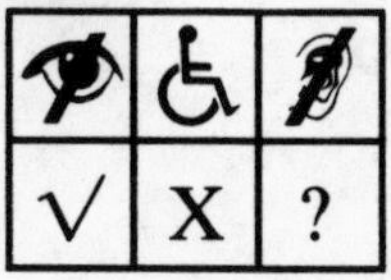

Belly Laughs

Numbers

Everybody (minimum 8–10)

Equipment

None

Details

Get everyone to lie on their backs with the back of their head on someone else's tummy.

If it is a small group, get the people to lie down one at a time in sequence — otherwise leave them to sort out whose tummy to lie on.

On the word 'go' the first person is instructed to call out 'HA' once. The person with head on that tummy calls 'HA, HA', and down the row in number order. When it fails, start again — or start at the other end.

End before it dies a death.

Special notes

Heads bob up and down as people 'Ha' or laugh uncontrollably.

6

👁	♿	🏃
?	?	✓

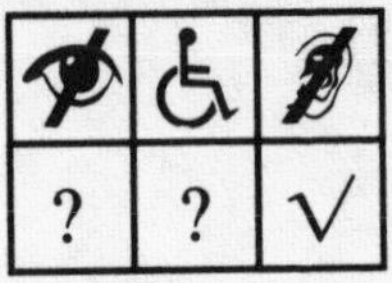

Birthday Row

Numbers

Everybody (minimum 8–10)

Equipment

None

Details

Ask everyone to form into groups of approximately 10 people. Ask the team to NON-VERBALLY put themselves in line according to *BIRTHDAY ORDER*. i.e. 1st January 1st etc.

Special notes

Emphasise that it is day and month only (not year). Have the winning group to call out their dates of birth and check it! Often it can be wrong. Affirm other groups' attempts.

But I've got two birthdays

7

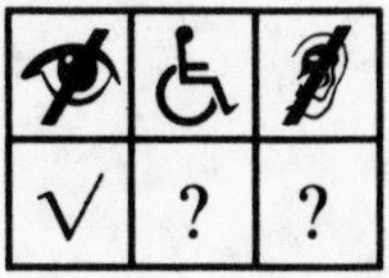

Rain maker

Numbers

Everybody (groups of 6–10)

Equipment

None

Details

This game is played without talking. Each member takes it in turns lying down in the centre of a circle formed by other members.
Relax, and close the eyes.
The leader then says the following:

'Rain drops begin to fall.' At this point, the group members tap slowly, with their forefingers *all* over the person's body.

'The rain becomes a shower.'
Tapping becomes faster.

'It becomes a downpour.'
Harder and faster.

'The rain fades.'
Appropriate fading to stop.
Finally change the volunteer and start again.

Special notes

This is a beautiful game that creates a lovely experience for all, giving and receiving non-verbal affirmation.
It is usually very relaxing.

8

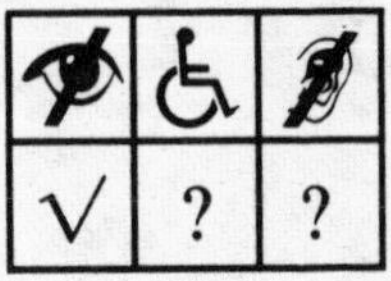

Animal Labels

Numbers

As many as the number of labels permits, preferably all present.

Equipment

Labels (self adhesive) with names of animals on e.g. Dog, Cat, Pig, Mouse, etc.

Details

Stick a label on each person's forehead — but don't show them.
They then go around asking questions, whose answers can only be yes or no.
Only one question to each person, e.g. Do I have four legs? Am I a cow?
The aim is to find out your animal and, even more importantly, to mix everyone up.

Special notes

This is a good icebreaker.
The labels could go on their backs instead of on their foreheads.

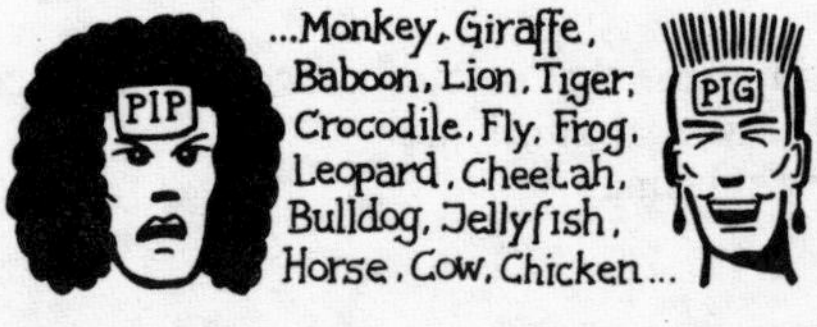

GETTING YOUR
HAND IN

9

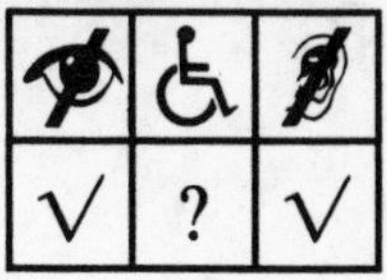
√ ? √

Getting Your Hand In

Numbers

Total participation in groups or one group of 6–10 people.

Equipment

None

Details

The group stands in a tight circle, with each one facing into the centre. Everyone puts their right hand into the centre, one on top of other. Then do the same with the left hand, so that we have a stack of hands. On the word 'go' the bottom hand is pulled out on to the top of pile, followed by the next — and so on.
(Good fun.)
The next phase is for the leader to give a pre-determined signal (e.g. blowing a whistle) and the stack automatically reverses.

Special notes

This is a good fun game, which teaches co-operation.

So much for
short people!

10

👁	♿	👂
√	X	√

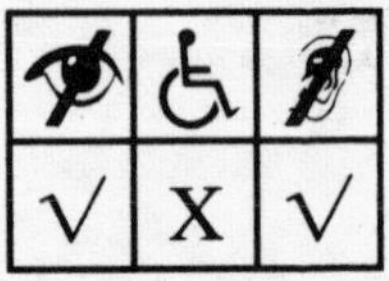

Get Knotted

Numbers

Total participation or one group of 6–10.

Equipment

None

Details

Form the group into a circle, shoulder to shoulder. Get them to mingle their hands in the centre of the circle. Each hand should then grab another — but not their neighbour's.

On the command 'go', untangle without letting go.

Special notes

This is a good contact game.
Expect lots of laughs.
It is not always possible to untie the circle.
Affirm, especially those who don't complete the game.
This game can often be repeated time and time again with no less fun.

I think this might be possible gang

11

👁️	♿	🏃
?	X	✓

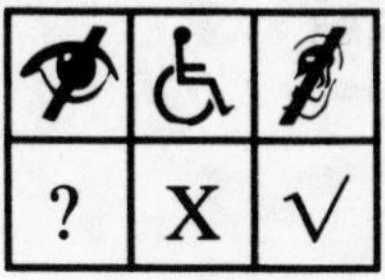

Clean T-Shirt

Numbers

Everybody in groups of 10–15

Equipment

Someone's T-shirt.

Details

Get everyone into groups of approximately ten, standing in a circle. Find a volunteer in each group to remove a T-shirt. Get the group to lay out the T-shirts neatly in the centre of group. Emphasise that we do not want to soil the T-shirt. Then get everyone to stand on the T-shirt.

The aim is to build a tower without anyone touching the floor.

Special notes

Get the wearer to remove the T-shirt, first.
It can be dangerous as the tower collapses.

RING-A-RING-A-ROSES

12

👁	♿	🏃
√	?	X

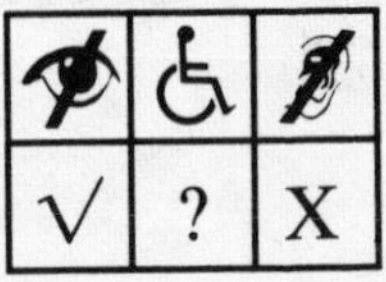

Ring-a-Ring-a-Roses

Numbers

About 6–10

Equipment

None

Details

Everyone gets into groups of 6–10, and forms a circle.
Everyone put arms around each other's shoulders in 'hug circle formation'.
Ask everyone to tell the person on their right one thing that they like about that person. Affirmation then goes round the circle.

Special notes

Encourage participants to try to do this without laughing and being too embarrassed.
We are not experienced enough at giving and receiving affirmation. It is most beneficial if the game is played with real openness and honesty.

CIRCLE OF TRUST

13

👁	♿	🏃
?	X	√

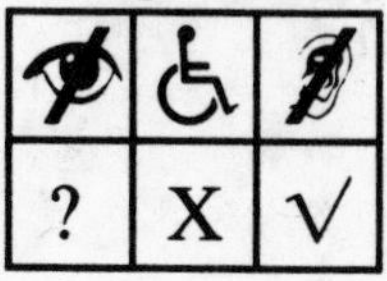

Circle of Trust

Numbers

Everybody (minimum of 20)

Equipment

None

Details

i. All except one person, stand in two circles.
ii. One circle, inside another circle, facing out.
iii. One circle, outside the other circle, facing in, so that everyone is facing a partner.
iv. Criss-cross hands with neighbour and partner.
v. Then in turn one person lies across the arms of the group and with the group lifting and bouncing a lovely ride can be enjoyed.

Special notes

i. Remove all watches and bracelets — anything loose or sharp from fingers, hands or arms.
ii. This game can be dangerous unless participants are in a mood of *trust*.
iii. Encourage participants to provide a positive experience of trust for each other.
iv. This can be done in a long line but participants must be caught at the end.

Mmm, so this is what being a model railway engine feels like...

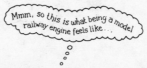

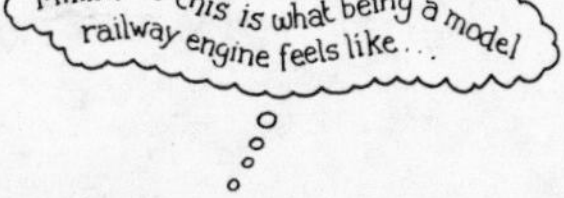

14

√	X	√

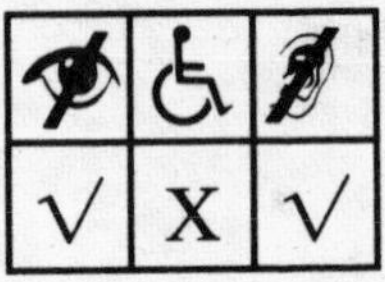

Head Balancing Act

Numbers

Everybody (minimum 8–10)

Equipment

Balloons for everyone.

Details

Issue balloons between two people and they inflate them.
Placing balloons between foreheads they are challenged to run around
the campsite/room.

Special notes

Watch for odd people out and encourage groups of threes if needed.
Emphasise the co-operative aspect.

Amazing, well done you two

STIFF AS A BOARD

15

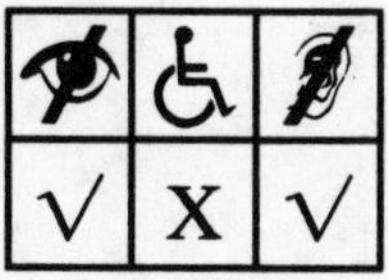

Stiff as a Board

Numbers

Everybody (minimum of 4 per group)

Equipment

None

Details

Get everyone into groups of 4 (or 5 if odd ones). Each group member in turn lies face down on the floor arms extended, feet together 'Stiff as a Board'. Other members of the group lift them off the floor (only 12 inches), with one at each arm and one at feet. The idea is to carry the person until they collapse into a heap.

Special notes

Watch for people being left out of groups, and encourage 5's if so. Emphasise *not* to lift people high!

Jenkins! Wilson is not a battering ram

16

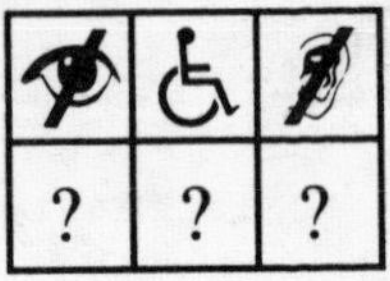

It's a Tick

Numbers

Everybody (minimum 8–10)

Equipment

None

Details

Get all into groups of approximately 10, sitting in tight circle with knees touching.
One person takes their shoes off and passes them to the right saying 'Here's a Tick'.
The person doesn't take it but says 'A what?'
The first person says 'A Tick!'
And *then* it's passed on. The second person holds it towards third person and says 'Here's a Tick'.
Third person says 'A what?'
and the question 'A what?' is passed back to the first person and then returns along the line 'A Tick!'
When game has got going *then* he/she takes another object (i.e. a pen) and passes it along the other way. Repeat the same procedure except that the words are 'Here's a Tock'.

Special notes

A demonstration by a group at the front can explain it better than words.
Expect confusion and laughter.

ELECTRIC SHOCK

17

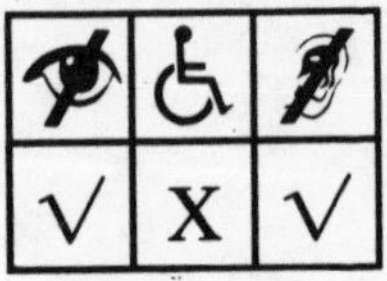

Electric Shock

Numbers

Everybody (minimum 8)

Equipment

None

Details

Get everyone into groups of approximately 10.
One member stands in the centre of a circle and the rest hold hands. On the word 'go' the group pulls circle so that another group member touches the 'live wire' at centre and therefore changes place.

Special notes

It's a good game to get a group livened up at the start of a meeting. Some people are not 'at home' with the roughness.

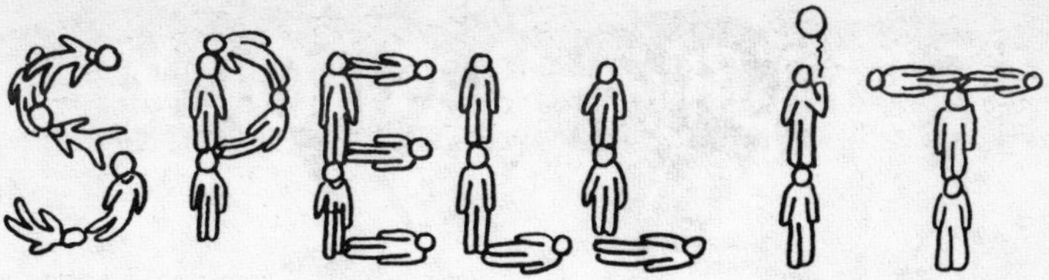

18

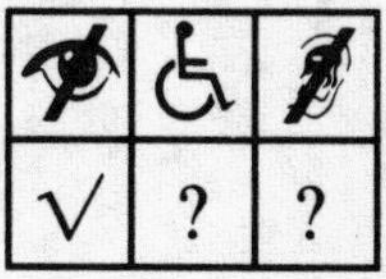

Spell It

Numbers

Everybody (minimum 25)

Equipment

None

Details

Get everyone into groups of 10 or so in a line and holding hands.
Count how many groups and decide on a word.
On the word 'go' the groups have to form a letter each that spells the word.
For example, 'Greenbelt' will need nine groups, with one group forming each letter.
Allow the group to decide how to do it, and watch the fun.

Special notes

This game encourages large group co-operation, and small group co-operation.
Repeat with other words but don't overdo it!
Alternative: shout out a number (say 6) and *each* group has to decide on a word and spell it, using their bodies.
This is more competitive, the other game is more co-operative.

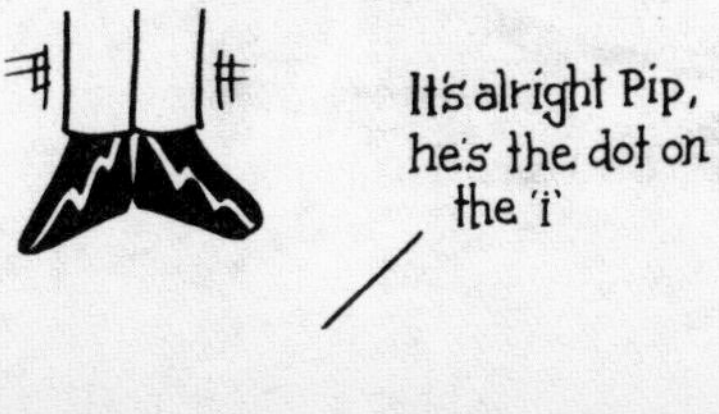

It's alright Pip, he's the dot on the 'i'

19

👁	♿	🏃
?	X	√

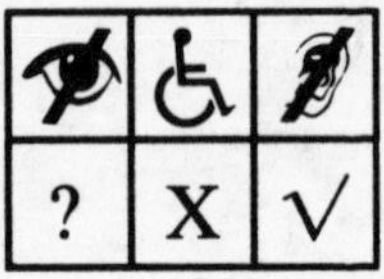

Bump Bums

Numbers

Everybody *or* all boys or all girls

Equipment

None

Details

Everyone holds both ankles with both hands, left ankle left hand etc. On the word 'go' everyone tries to knock the others over, without letting go of ankles and using *only* 'bums'.

Special notes

A mad boisterous game.
Be sensitive, stop before it becomes too rough or boring.

Don't forget
the pillows

20

👁	♿	🏃
√	?	√

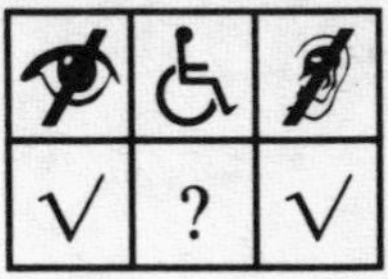

Hug Circle

Numbers

Everybody

Equipment

None

Details

Get all present into circles of approximately 10 people. Ask the people if they remember 'Get Knotted' (see game 10, they may have played it previously).

Pretend you are about to replay it but instead get everyone to put arms over each other's shoulders in a linked circle. Count down and on 'go' everyone invited to give the group a big group hug.

Ask them to share how it feels then re-play.

Join more groups together, if appropriate, and end with all those present having a big group hug.

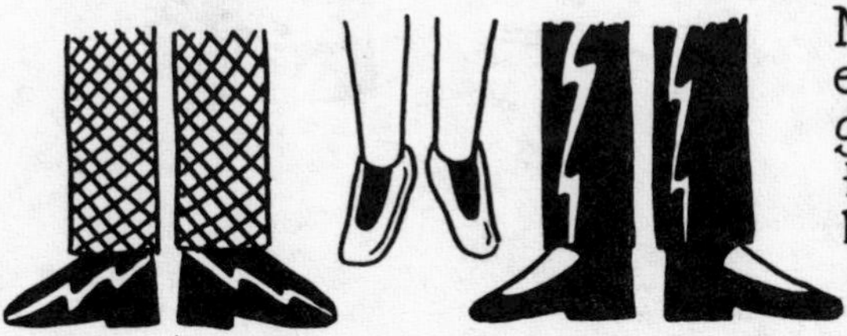

Make sure everyone in the group is about the same height

21

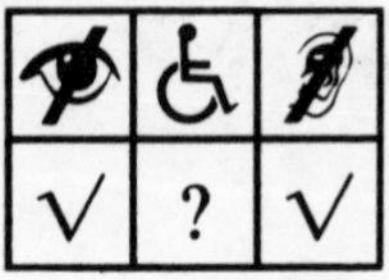

Game for a Laugh

Numbers

Teams of 10

Equipment

None

Details

Get groups to a line up of five facing five, having mixed sexes is wise; standing a few feet apart. Have them letter themselves either A or B on the word 'go': the A Team must *not* laugh, and B Team must laugh. If they break the rule they swop sides.
Find the champion teams and get them to play each other.

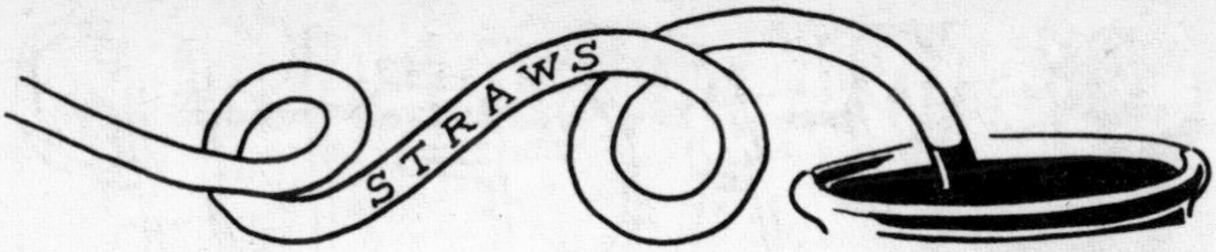

22

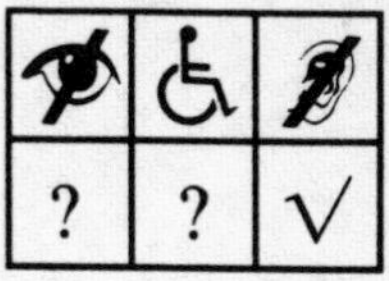

Straws

Numbers

Everybody

Equipment

A box of plastic drinking straws.

Details

Game 1. Form groups into teams of 6–10 with one straw per team. On the word ‘go’ the team pass down the straw along the line by only holding the straws between their nose and top lip.

Game 2. Everyone gets a straw and holds one end in their mouth and hands placed behind back.
On ‘go’ everyone has to transfer their grip from one end of straw to the other.

Game 3. Everyone gets a straw and holds one end in their mouth and places hands behind back. On ‘go’ everyone has to chew the straw so that it is all inside the mouth.

Game 4. Stand a large litter bin in the middle of a circle of participants. On ‘go’ the olympic javelin competition is held to see who can throw the straw javelin into the bin.

You see there's so many things to do with your common straw

?	X	✓

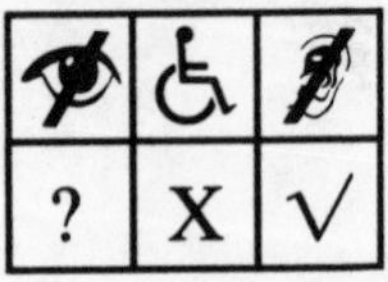

Lace Up

Numbers

Everybody

Equipment

None

Details

Get everyone into groups of 10 to 15 and stand in a circle. Everyone takes off their shoes and piles them in centre. On the word 'go' the group moves away to another pile of shoes nearby. On 'go two' the group tie all the shoe laces together in knots. On 'go three' they pick up the pile and mingle around with other groups and deposit them in another part of the field/hall. On 'go four' everyone runs and the first team back with all their shoes on and laced up wins.

Special notes

Really good game to play following other group games.

I've won

24

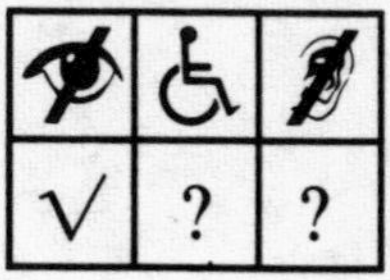

Making Rain

Numbers

Everybody

Equipment

None

Details

Get everyone with you sitting down and agree to make rain.

Stage 1. Everyone practises clicking their thumb and second finger out of sequence.

Stage 2. Everyone practises rubbing their palms together fast.

Stage 3. Everyone practises patting their knees or thighs with the flat of their hands.

Stage 4. Everyone practises patting feet on the floor.

Stage 5. Divide everyone into groups of four and each group takes one item (1 to above).

On the word 'go' everyone does their bit and you MAKE RAIN.

See following page for **Special Notes**

Special notes

Experiment.
Raise hand louder rain — a storm!
Lower hand quiet rain — a shower!
Run your hand over length of the whole group and you can send the rain from one end all the way along out of the door!!!!
Great with a really big crowd.

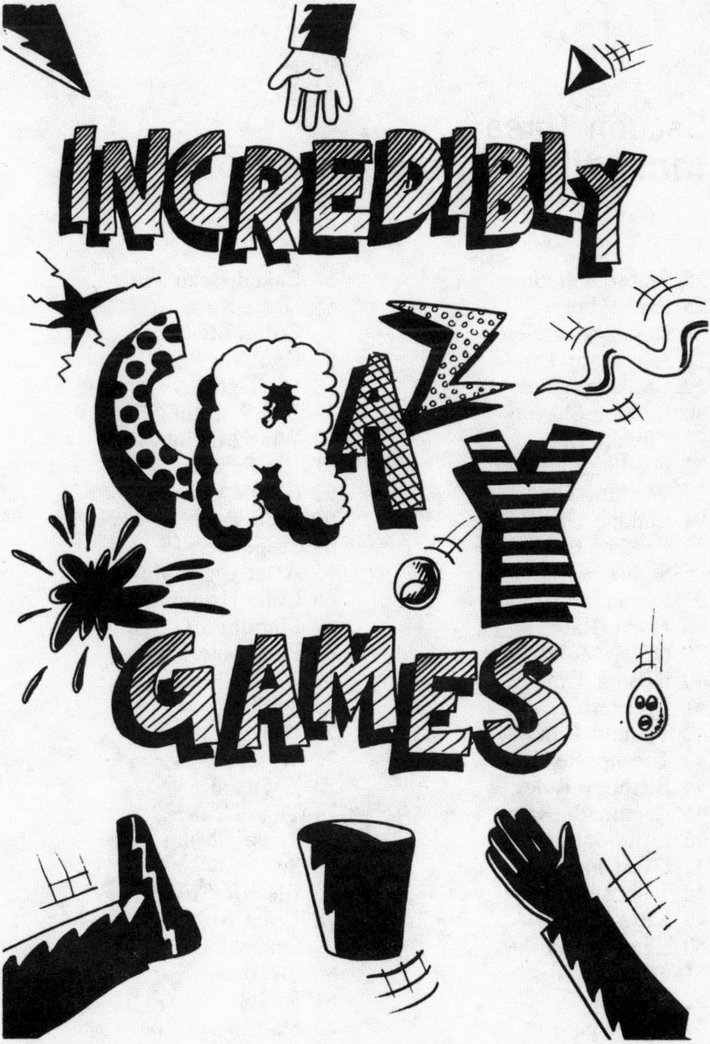
INCREDIBLY
CRAZY
GAMES

Section Three
Incredibly Crazy Games

25 Water Balloon
26 Party Hair
27 Russian Omelette
28 Jelly Baby Dip
29 Choke a Yoke
30 Balloon Shavers
31 Chucky Egg
32 Feeding the Blind
33 Washing Day
34 Making-Up
35 Feeding the Baby
36 Squirt
37 Father Christmas
38 Horse Race
39 Minty Mouth
40 Kissing Time
41 Cracker
42 Tomato Run
43 Toothpaste Drop
44 Birthday Ruler
45 Lemonade Race
46 Little Squirt
47 Chest Face
48 Tombstone
49 Sieve Head
50 Egg Cup Kissing
51 Thriller
52 Porridge
53 Knickers
54 Baked-Bean Trifle
55 Dress Race
56 Coffin Measure
57 Knobbly Eggs
58 Up Tights
59 Egg Wrestling
60 Wine Making
61 10p Funnel
62 Gargle Queen
63 Feed Face
64 Suspenders
65 After Eight Mints
66 Coke Drinking Contest
67 Marathon Gargle
68 Porcupine Pass
69 Bubble Yum
70 3^z Chain
71 Foot Sign
72 Water Feet
73 Egg Roll
74 Tug of Peace
75 Smile a Mile
76 Suddenly
77 Electric Chair
78 Team Roll
79 One Minute Shower
80 Li-Lo
81 Rudolf
82 Skip to the Loo

25

👁	♿	🏃
?	?	✓

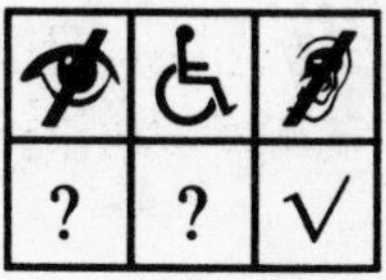

Water Balloon Toss

Numbers

2 couples, or more, the more the better.

Equipment

A balloon filled with water for each couple.

Details

Couples face each other in lines 3 feet apart. On the word 'go' the balloon is thrown to a partner who catches it, steps one pace back and returns the balloon.
The process continues until all balloons have burst.

Special notes

The audience back away from this one as spectacular throwing and catching often ensues. It is a good game for outdoors or campsites.

Ideal for sport photography

PARTY HAIR

26

👁️	♿	🦻
√	√	√

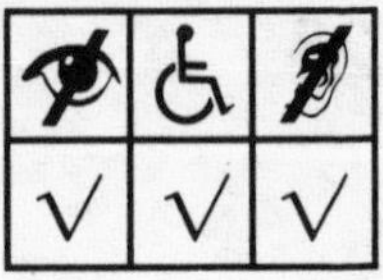

Party Hair

Numbers

2 or 3 couples

Equipment

Per couple:
aerosol party streamers, in various colours.

Details

The boys sit down on a chair with a girl behind them, on the word 'go' the girls design hairdos on the boy's head, aiming to do the best design with eye brows, sideburns and even moustaches.

Special notes

Warn the boys to keep their eyes closed.
The can needs a good shake before and during the game.
The game can also be played with the girls blindfolded.
This is a good game for the audience to enjoy.

Youthful Pride

RUSSIAN OMLETTE

27

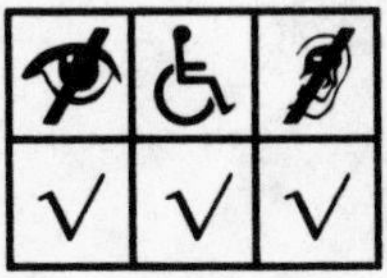

Russian Omelette

Numbers

3 couples, or more, up to a maximum of 6 couples

Equipment

Per couple: 1 egg.

Details

Seat the boys on a chair facing the audience.
The girls stand behind them with one palm open flat.
Instructions given, with a big build-up.
The audience are told that all the eggs are boiled (carefully boiled and not cracked) except one (in fact only boil half of the eggs for extra effect).

Special notes

Often there are complaints from boiled egg couples.
And they can be offered an extra raw egg to avoid disappointment.
The audience love it!
Build up the fun before the start.
Isn't it eggciting!!

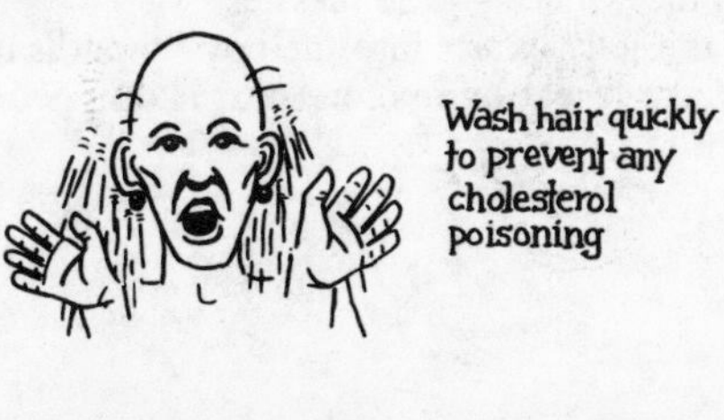
Wash hair quickly
to prevent any
cholesterol
poisoning

JELLY BABY DIP

28

√	?	√

Jelly Baby Dip

Numbers

3 couples are best

Equipment

3 packets of Jelly Babies.
3 plastic water cups.
3 cups of chocolate dip or sauce.
3 paper towels.

Details

The girls stand on chairs above the boys' heads who are holding cups in their mouths while lying on backs.
On the word 'go' the girls dip Jelly Baby in chocolate and drop the sweet into the cup. (It often misses!) When all 'babies' are dropped the girls are encouraged to pour the remaining chocolate at the same target.

Special notes

It is a messy game but the better for it.
Only use towels if the dress warrants it!
Give a prize to the winner — the messiest!!
Variation drop the jelly babies into the boys' mouths instead of in the cups and they have to eat one before next is dropped.

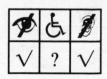

OK, so there's only chocolate bars Bina, but you could at least take the wrapper off

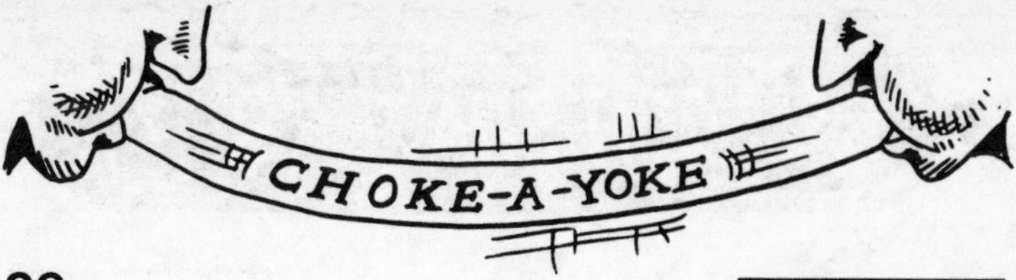

29

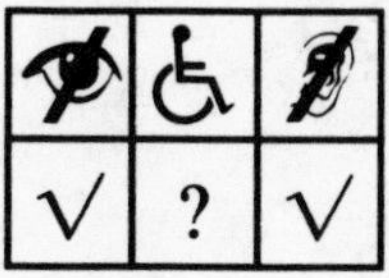

Choke a Yoke

Numbers

2 people

Equipment

1 length of clear plastic tube 4 feet long with ¾″ bore.
Small funnel.
A raw egg.

Details

Men or women, boys or girls can play.
Have two volunteers come up. Build this as a most ghastly game and only for the strong, self-willed, well-educated, good looking and those who possess good teeth (all which have no significance).
Produce the first piece of equipment, the tube; instruct the volunteers to hold one end each at head height in full view of audience. Then produce the next piece of equipment, the egg and show it off to audience. With big build-up, place the funnel in one end and demonstratively crack the egg into the funnel and allow it to run into the centre of tube. The volunteers then both place lips at each end and on the word 'go' they blow! Eventually one gets the yolk!

Special notes

The audience love it!
Give lots of encouragement to the volunteers.

30

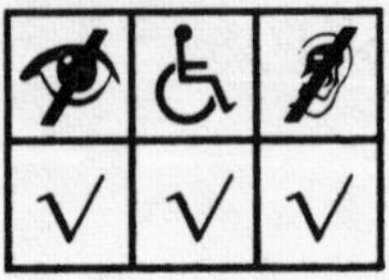

Balloon Shavers

Numbers

3 couples

Equipment

3 balloons (you will need a few spares).
3 razors.
3 cans of shaving cream.

Details

The boys sit on chairs, facing the audience.
The girls stand behind the chairs.
Each boy has balloon in his mouth (held in the teeth not literally in mouth!!).
The girls cover the balloons with shaving cream.
On the word 'go' the girls shave the balloon while music is playing.

Special notes

A game which often ends with no balloons bursting, but the anticipation is good audience stuff. At the end, secretly give the girls a pin each and on 'go' they burst the balloon (the girls get as much scattered foam as the boys!).

![eye]	![wheelchair]	![thrown]
X	?	√

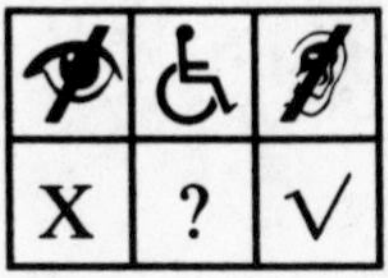

Chucky Egg

Numbers

3 couples, or more

Equipment

1 egg per couple.

Details

Each couple faces each other in lines 3 feet apart.
One person from each couple is given an egg and on the word 'go' they throw it to partner.
On catching each person steps back one pace before passing it back to partner.
Couples drop out as eggs are shattered.

Special notes

The audience dive for cover.
Make sure the venue can stand this game.
School or Church Hall caretakers may not appreciate 'the fun'.
This is a good game for outdoors — fete, camps etc.
Recommended to start a good games session.
It starts the evening off with eggcitement!!

PACIFISM
AND
THE EGG

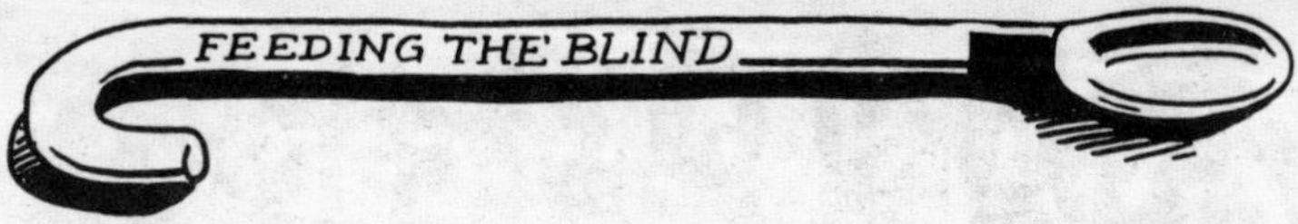

32

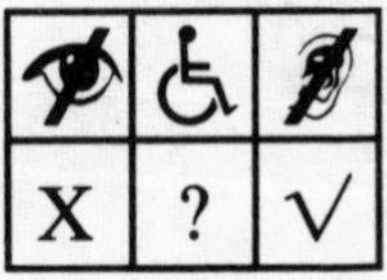

Feeding the Blind

Numbers

3 couples

Equipment

6 bowls of food.
6 blindfolds.
6 large plastic spoons, as large as possible.

Details

Sit couples side by side along one side of a trestle table, facing the audience. Give them a spoon each and place before them a bowl of cornflakes. Say it is race to eat all cornflakes and can only feed each other not feed oneself. Say ready steady 'g . . . .', pause, and say you forgot a vital piece of equipment then produce the blindfolds.
Fit them and 'go'.

Special notes

1. *For extra fun* have items ready to add to the bowls e.g. lumps of bread, mustard pickle, tomato sauce.
2. *Similar game* give couples teeth cleaning instruments and get them to clean each other's teeth.
3. *Warning* warn against breaking teeth!

WASHING DAY

33

👁	♿	👂
√	?	√

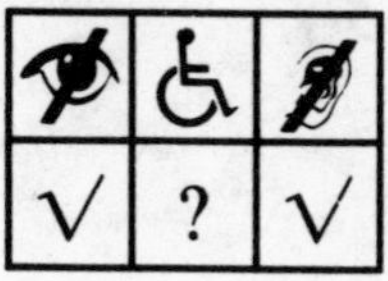

Washing Day

Numbers

1 couple, or more if sufficient equipment

Equipment

2 bags full of colourful clothes pegs.
2 blindfolds.

Details

Play this for the length of a record, about 3–4 minutes, or until the first finishes.
Couples stand facing the audience, and are given bag of pegs each.
Instructions are to peg as many on the other as possible.
Introduce the blindfold at the last minute, to complicate things!

So this is how Joan Collins feels

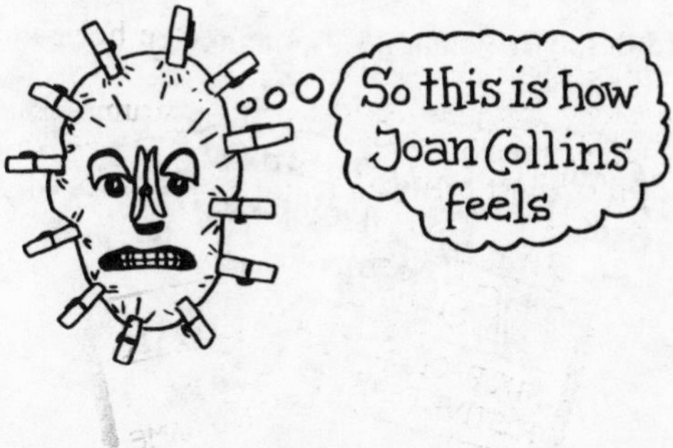

MAKING UP

34

?	?	√

Making-Up

Numbers

2 couples, or more if equipment allows

Equipment

Blindfold, cream 'make-up' remover.
Make-up sets, e.g. lipstick, blusher, powder, liner etc.
Chairs.
Trestle table.

Details

The boys sit on one side of table, facing the audience.
The girls stand behind their partners.
The object of the game is for the women (with blindfolds on) to 'make-up' their partner.
Introduce the blindfolds at the last minute — it creates *extra* fun.

Special notes

Play a record during the game (3 — 4 minutes).

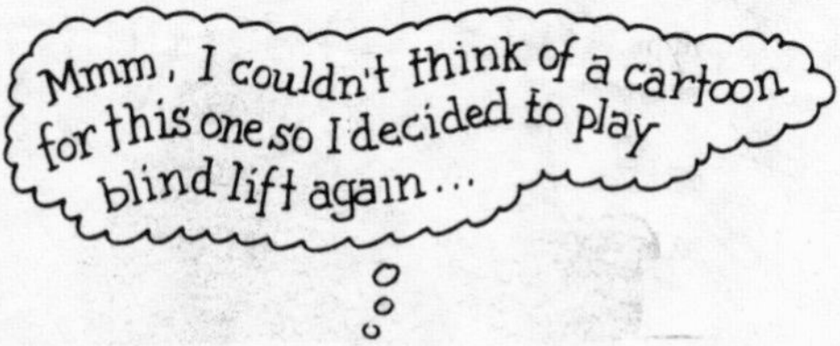

Mmm, I couldn't think of a cartoon for this one so I decided to play blind lift again...

35

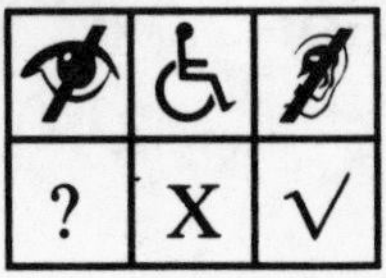

Feeding the Baby

Numbers

2 couples, or more

Equipment

2 baby bottles and teats.
2 cans of lemonade.
2 baby bibs.
2 baby nappies (towels) and pins.

Details

Get the girls to dress up the boys baby-style.
Females have a bottle and a can of lemonade each and holding their bottles they seat their partner on their laps and feed them. They empty the can of drink into the bottle and the one who drinks it the fastest wins.

Special notes

Prize for the winner — they can keep the bibs.

SQUIRT

36

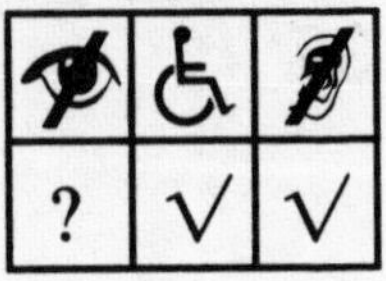

Squirt

Numbers

3 couples

Equipment

3 cans of shaving foam.
3 water pistols.
Water.
Towels.

Details

Boys sit on chairs, facing audience.
Girls put a big blob of foam onto their partner's nose.
On the word 'go' they SQUIRT it off with water pistol from a distance of 10 feet.

Special notes

Use towels to protect boys (if necessary).
Ideal for a Summer Camp.

Go for it Phil, I haven't had a wash all week!

37

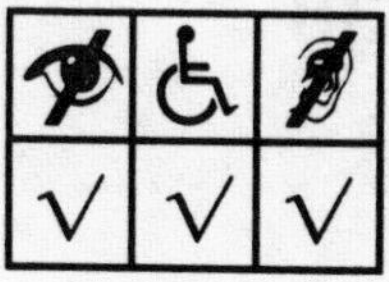

Father Christmas

Numbers

Couples, 3 boys and 3 girls

Equipment

3 chairs.
3 blindfolds.
3 cans of shaving foam.
Washing facilities, or wet-ones.
(3 Father Christmas outfits, if possible)

Details

The boys sit in chairs facing the audience.
The girls stand at their side blindfolded with a can of shaving foam.
On the word 'go' the girls are to design the best Father Christmas face with beard, eyebrows, etc.

Special notes

Warn the boys to keep eyes shut and be prepared to help clean up stinging eyes.
Judge them all winners and encourage audience appreciation.
This is a good Christmas party game.
Red coats helps the atmosphere.
Married women seem to love doing this to their husbands. Try the Vicar and his wife!

HORSE RACE

![eye]	![wheelchair]	![lightning]
?	X	?

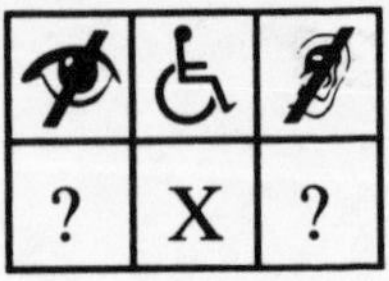

Horse Race

Numbers

2 couples, or more

Equipment

2 eggs.
2 blindfolds.

Details

Boys become the horse and the girls jump on their backs. Instructions are given regarding the obstacle course.
Say you will count down 5 4 3 2 1 GO.
Just before go, produce boys' blindfolds — the girls have to give directions to the blind horse.
Say 5 4 3 2 1 STOP!
Just before GO!
Remember that girls have to hold an egg between their teeth.
5 4 3 2 1 GO!

Special notes

Run around marquee poles or whatever the hurdles.
Ask the audience to stay where they are and *not* move out of their way.
A good audience game, they love it when the egg breaks down the boy's neck!

Yes, and you're the horse

39

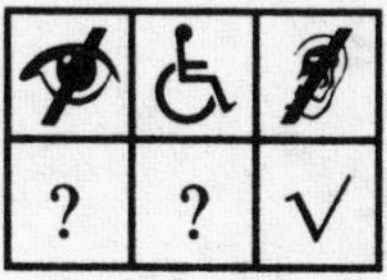

Minty Mouth

Numbers

3 couples

Equipment

6 tubes of Polo mints.

Details

The contestants face the audience.
The aim is for one partner to put as many Polos as possible in their partner's mouth (no eating or swallowing).
Have the audience in 3 sections, count as they are put in the mouths.

Special notes

It is amazing how many go in!
A good prize is a packet of Polos.

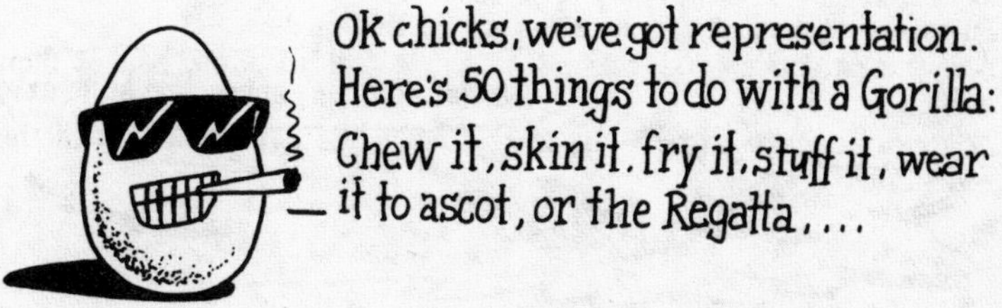

OK chicks, we've got representation.
Here's 50 things to do with a Gorilla:
Chew it, skin it, fry it, stuff it, wear it to ascot, or the Regatta, ...

KISSING TIME

40

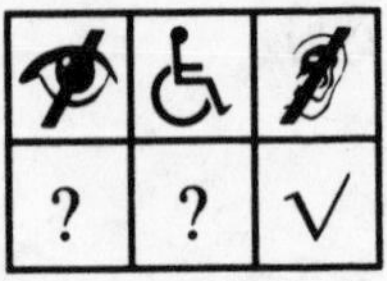
?
?
√

Kissing Time

Numbers

3 couples

Equipment

3 tubes of bright red lipstick.
3 blindfolds.

Details

Using as many couples as you want, blindfold the girls and with a lipstick in their mouths they have to apply lipstick to boys' lips. No hand contact from either of them is allowed.

Special notes

Sellotape lipsticks to 'out' position.
Hands behind the backs is best.
If appropriate have girls kiss a boy with lipstick on.
The audience love it!

So, Gorillas can't appreciate humour

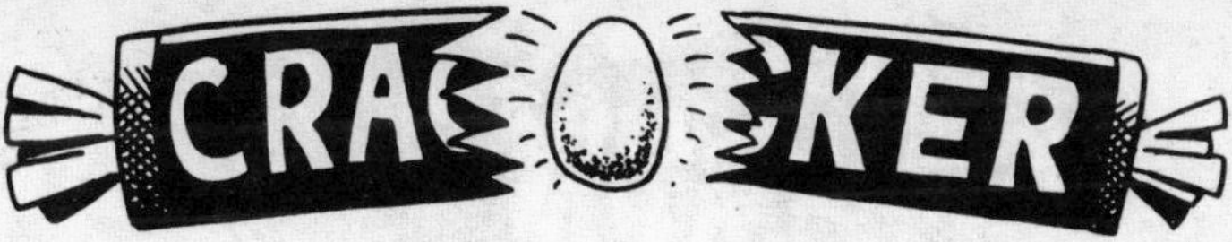

41

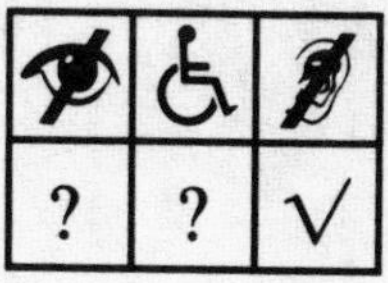

Cracker

Numbers

3 couples

Equipment

3 eggs.
3 plastic cups.
3 stools.
Tissues.
Washing facilities.

Details

The girls stand on stools facing the audience.
The boys lie down on their backs with their heads just in front of the stools.
The boys are given plastic cups to put in their mouths. Then, with ceremony, the equipment is brought out — the eggs.
On the word 'go' the girls must crack the eggs and drop the contents into the cups from the full height.

Special notes

All participants are winners and the audience are asked to show their appreciation and enjoy the 'damage' done.
Often the eggs 'splatter' in all directions.

TOMATO
RUN

42

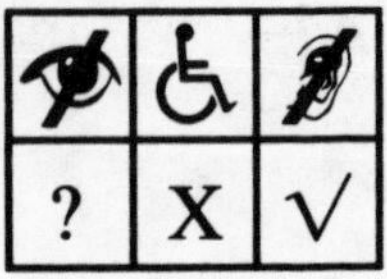

Tomato Run

Numbers

2 couples, although better with 3

Equipment

A tomato per couple, plus spares.

Details

Line up the participants for the best audience view.
Couples place the tomato between their foreheads. On the word 'go' they bend down and remove each other's shoes and then run to a marker, 5 yards out, and return and put their shoes back on their feet.

Special notes

The audience are encouraged to applaud the failures i.e. the squashed tomatoes.

And to think - all because of a tomato!

43

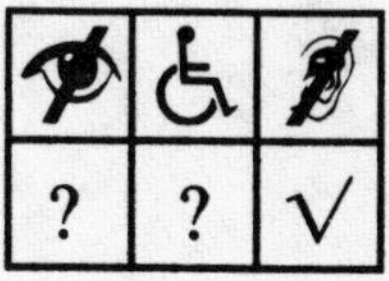

Toothpaste drop

Numbers

3 couples

Equipment

3 small tubes of toothpaste.
3 plastic cups.
Tissues and washing facilities.

Details

The girls stand on stools facing the audience. The boys on their backs, lie with their heads near the stools with cups in their mouths.
With ceremony the girls are presented with tubes of toothpaste.
On the word 'go' the girls squeeze tubes to transfer the paste into the plastic cups.
On completion show off the results to the audience and ask them for a show of appreciation.

Special notes

Boys warned to keep eyes tightly shut or provide tissue blindfolds.

No! Kate, you drop the toothpaste not the tube
COUGH
CHOKE

44

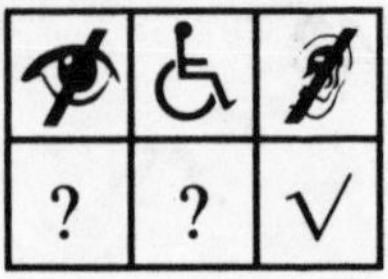

Birthday Ruler

Numbers

2 couples, although better with 3

Equipment

Per couple:
12″ ruler.
Small candle stuck on one end with Blutak.
Water pistol.
Matches.
Towels.
3 stools.

Details

The boys sit on the stools facing audience.
Rulers are placed in their mouths and the candles are lit.
On the word 'go' girls, from a suitable distance, are to squirt out the flame.

Special notes

Check all pistols are equally good and full.

45

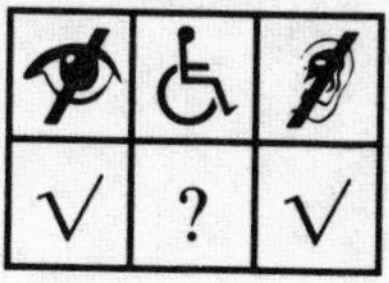

Lemonade Race

Numbers

3 people although better with 4

Equipment

Per person:
1 lemon.
One-quarter cup of sugar.
1 cup of water.
1 empty lemonade bottle.

Details

Announce the lemonade drinking contest!
Contestants stand behind a table. A big build-up is given about the speed and consumption of lemonade. Three empty bottles are placed on table and the build-up continues until someone notices there is no lemonade!
The team are asked for an alternative and lemons are produced, followed by sugar and water.
On the word 'go' the contestants are encouraged to eat the lemonade.

Special notes

This will be a race that can continue during the playing of a record. Encourage the fun aspect and encourage all the contestants.

The second part of the race . . .

46

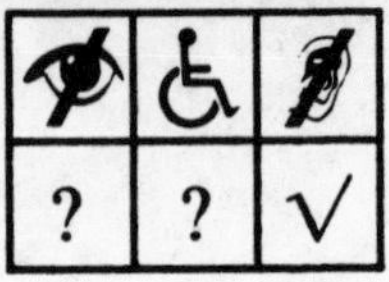

Little Squirt

Numbers

2 couples although better with 3

Equipment

Per couple:
2 waterpistols.
2 blindfolds.
1 powerful garden spray gun filled with water.

Details

Courting couples are best for this — they can take it!
Give both the boy and the girl a water pistol each and stand them out in the centre of hall.
Give instructions that this is a water pistol fight.
Just before 'go' remember the blindfolds!
Blindfold both and make sure the girls are blind-folded first.
Continue to give instructions about aiming blind in response to when you get 'hit' (while at the same time secretly remove the girls' blindfold and replace the water pistol with powerful jet spray).
On the word 'go' the girl has an incredible time spraying the boy leaving him 'no' chance.

Special notes

The audience love this.
At the end remove boys' blindfold so that the boys get the full shock of discovering the girls' advantage.

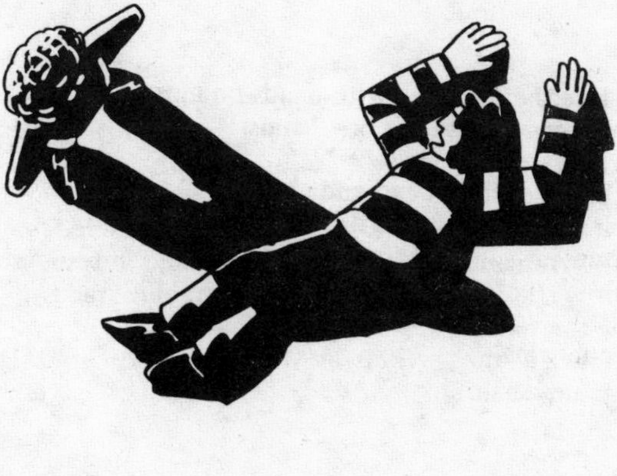

47

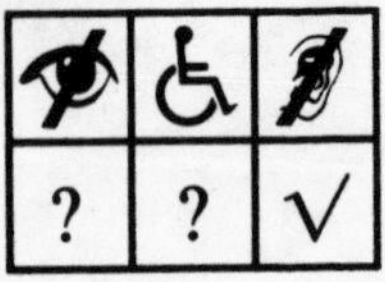

Chest Face

Numbers

2 boys
2 girls

Equipment

2 aprons with ties (painted or stitched on).
2 large hats (see the picture details).
2 sets of make-up — red and black.
1 jar of 'make-up' removal cream.

Details

The boys face the audience with hands on hips.
Place the aprons around the boys' waist.
Get them to bare their chests.
Put large hat *over* their head and shoulders.
Using their *natural* chest bits draw a large funny face.
Belly Button = Mouth
Nipples = Eyes
Arms = Ears
The best one wins.

Special notes

Keep artists to one side as they draw to enable the audience see the work in progress.
Well worth the trouble of making special hats and aprons — use a thick type of material.

The return of Bill and Ben

48

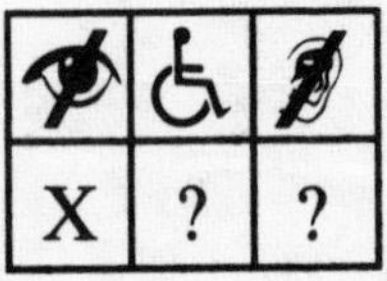

Tombstone

Numbers

Everybody

Equipment

1 piece of paper each.
1 pencil or pen.

Details

The aim is to stimulate humourous creative writing that also gives 'how they are seen by others' clues to participants.

1. Ask everyone to get into twos (and be sensitive to those around them because there may be at least one pair with 3 members!).
2. Ask them all to compose a tombstone for their partner which is both descriptive and funny using only a few words.
3. Ask them not to read out the finished product until the leader gives the word 'Go'.
4. Have them read out the summary to their partners and see the laughter around the room.

A sample:

Here lies the body of *Tubby Wilson*,
cuddly, cheerful chappy whose waistline
outgrew his brain. He leaves behind lots
of beautiful people and even more U2
records. His words he takes to his grave:
'STINKIN' EK!'

Special notes

An alternative is to write out a small advertisement for the local paper to 'sell' the person cheap!

'*For Sale* . . . worn out kisser, cuddly but thick . . .' etc.

49

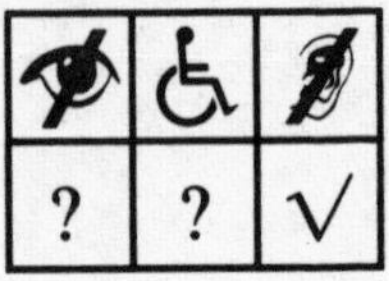

Sieve Head

Numbers

3 couples

Equipment

Per couple:
1 colander.
1 small tin of tomatoes.
1 egg.
1 stool.
1 bag of flour.
Washing facilities.

Details

The girls stand on stools facing the audience.
The boys hold a colander on top of their head in front of girls. They are instructed that they must run a circuit around the tent (or campsite) and return each time for the next addition to their colander.
With ceremony the first piece of equipment is brought out (the flour) and on the word 'go' the contents are emptied into the colander. The boys run; the audience love it. The boys return to their partners for the next item. First flour, second raw eggs and finally a third tin of tomatoes.

Special notes

This game is very popular in the 'right' environment. Popular with audience and participants. A big build-up, saying this game is really bad, will create a flood of volunteers to play 'sieve head' even though they haven't seen it.

Author's note. I've just received a request to play this at a wedding to entertain the congregation, while the couple are signing the register!

SANITY WARNING
ONLY A FOOL, A FOOL'S FRIEND,
OR HIS DOG, NORMALLY PLAY

EGG CUP KISSING

50

?	?	√

Egg Cup Kissing

Numbers

3 couples

Equipment

3 egg cups each attached to string.
3 eggs.
3 tomatoes.

Details

The girls stand on the stage.
The boys stand out in the audience — 15 feet away from the stage.
An egg cup is tied on top of boys' heads, like a cap.
The girls throw a tomato each in turn — throwing it high — the boys (try) to catch it in the egg cup.
For the next round, the girls throw the eggs.
It's a cracker.

Special notes

Like most games a 'big build-up' is needed to get the audience 'into' the game.

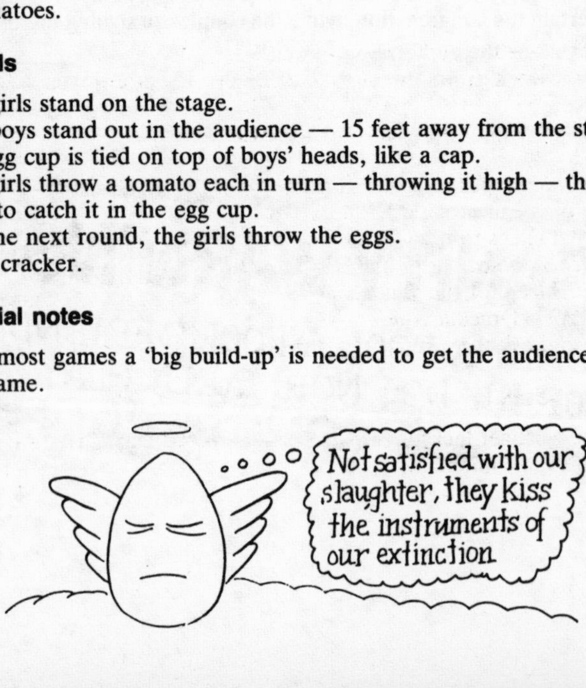

Not satisfied with our slaughter, they kiss the instruments of our extinction

THRILLER

51

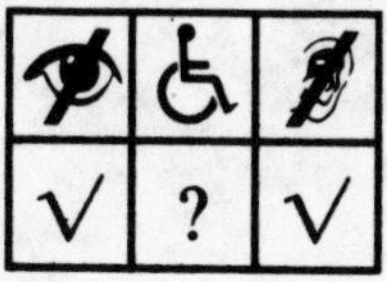

Thriller

Numbers

3 couples

Equipment

See below.

Details

The boys face the audience sat on chairs.
The girls work from the side to help the visual enjoyment of the audience.
The girls make-up the boys into werewolves, with:
Face packs.
Cotton balls to put into the mouth.
Peanut butter to provide texture!
Paint that sticks to dough (red and white).
Table tennis balls, cut in half, for the eyes.
Cocktail sticks for the whiskers.
False teeth – Dracula type.
At the end ask the girls to kiss her boyfriend!!

Special notes

Play the Michael Jackson 'Thriller' single record during the playing of the game (3–4 minutes).

52

?	?	√

Porridge

Numbers

3 or 4 couples

Equipment

Per couple:
Large clear plastic funnel.
Clear plastic tube 12″ long × 1½″ bore.
Jug of porridge.
List of questions — see below.

Details

Have 3 jugs of cold porridge standing ready.
Get the volunteers, ideally boy and girlfriends in couples.
Boys (or girls) grip the lip of funnel in mouth.
The tube is fixed to end with other end of tube tucked into the trousers.
Questions are asked and if participants get it wrong, or say 'pass' their girlfriend (or boyfriend) gives them the porridge.

Suggested questions for participants:
1. (i) What colour is a red bus?
   (ii) What colour is a brown owl?
   (iii) What colour is green grass?

2. (i) What was the name of the Indian who killed General Custer?
   (ii) What is the name of Pip's tortoise?
   It may be worth adding when the wrong answer is given, I haven't got one!!
   (iii) How many spots on a leopard?

Special notes

This game is good to build up to, advertise it, delay it, build great expectations.
Make people keen to volunteer! Make sure the porridge is runny enough (it is more interesting if it is coloured red or blue with food dye).
The audience love this.
Make sure people stand in a good position for maximum effect.
Think up your own relevant 'easy' and 'impossible' questions.
A participant wearing shorts adds to the fun!!

NO PORRIDGE - NO COMMENT

53

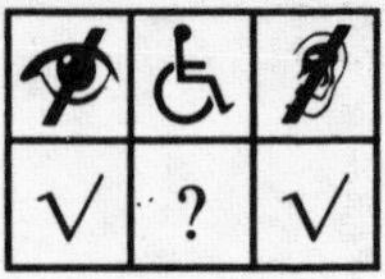

Knickers

Numbers

3 couples

Equipment

3 pairs of the largest old-fashioned knickers.
At least 60 balloons.

Details

Have the volunteers face the audience and put on the knickers.
On the word 'go' the other partner is given a load of balloons to blow up. (They can receive audience help.)
The partner stuffs as many balloons as possible into the knickers — from the top, back and up the legs too!
On conclusion, the leader counts the number of balloons, with the audience counting too, by using a pin to bust each balloon in turn.

Special notes

Good game for the audience and is very photogenic.
As many as 25 balloons can be stuffed per person.
It's an extra laugh to include a water balloon in each pile!

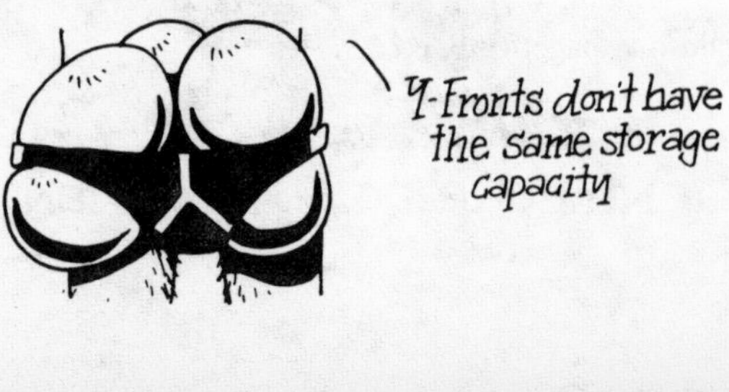

Y-Fronts don't have the same storage capacity

54

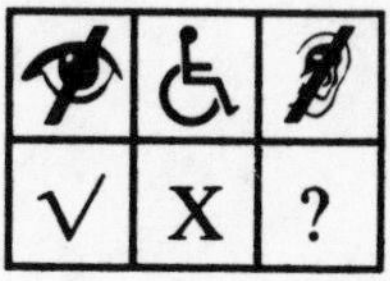

Baked-Bean Trifle

Numbers

3 couples

Equipment

3 very large clear funnels.
3 short lengths of clear hose (12″ fit on end of funnels).
3 clear plastic jugs.
Cleaning up materials.
Baked-Bean Trifle.

Details

Make sure you get real volunteers for this one.
It needs a big build-up; best used at the end of games session.
The boy stands on chair behind his mate who holds the lip of the funnel between her teeth.
Tuck end of hose down the front of upper garment.
With much ceremony hand the Baked-Bean Trifle to the boys.
Questions are then asked to the girls and when the answer is wrong or the word 'pass' is used the Trifle is demonstratively poured into the funnel.
The audience love it.

See following page for **Special Notes**

Special notes

You could do a preliminary round using water! It's good to do a round of very simple easy to answer questions, followed then by impossible to answer questions.

Ingredients for Baked-Bean Trifle
1 Tin Large Family Size Baked Beans
1 Packet Instant Custard (water based)
1 Packet Dream Topping (water based)
1 Cherry!

DRESS
RACE

55

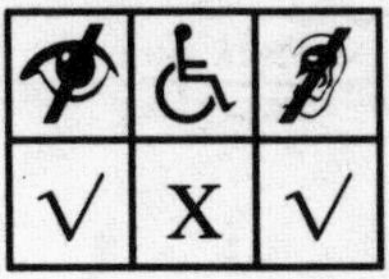
√
X
√

Dress Race

Numbers

2 or 3 couples

Equipment

2 pairs of Long Johns (white).
2 pairs of French Knickers.
2 Suspender Belts.
2 Brassieres.
2 cardboard boxes to put them in.
Red or Black

Details

Have 3 couples volunteer and have them face the audience.
On the word 'go' the girls are instructed to 'dress' the boys in the costume enclosed . . . (Make sure the Long Johns are on top of the box.) When 'dressed' they have to race outside around the tent (building) you are in and first one back gets a prize (a kiss from a girlfriend!).

Special notes

Very good for the audience but a shock to the public outside! I will be talked about amongst a group of friends for weeks.

I'd like to play, only
I don't know what
half the equipment
means Pip

COFFIN MEASURE

56

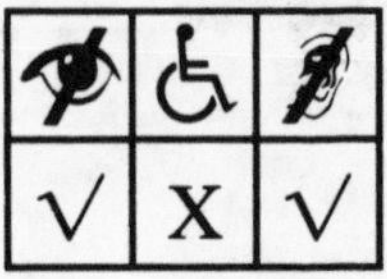
√ X √

Coffin Measure

Numbers

1 victim, 2 helpers male or female in trousers

Equipment

Tape measure.
Cup of water.

Details

Lay the volunteer on a table (or floor).
The victim's eyes must be closed.
Introduce this as a dead person — deceased.
The aim is to measure the person for a coffin.
Be precise in measuring head, shoulders, arms, length.
The climax is lifting the leg up to measure length and then . . . a cup of water is poured down it.

Special notes

The chat is very important.

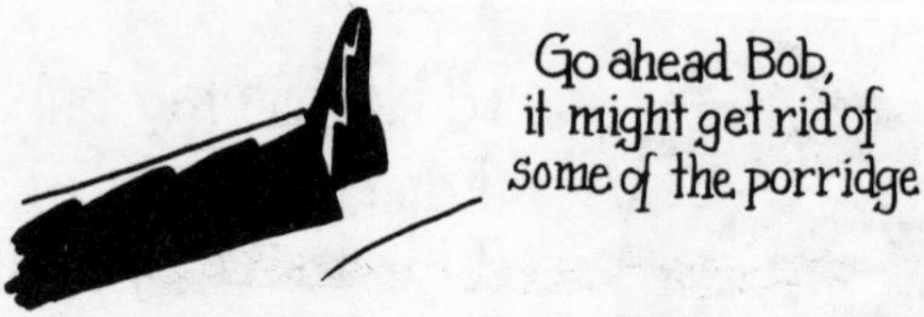
Go ahead Bob,
it might get rid of
some of the porridge

![eye]	![wheelchair]	![lightning]
?	X	√

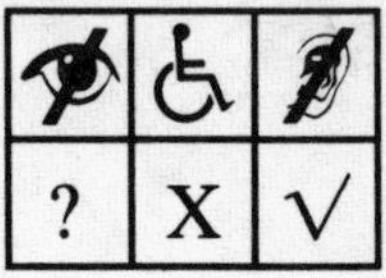

Knobbly Eggs

Numbers

3 or 4 volunteers

Equipment

2 eggs per person.

Details

Describe this as a race around the tent/campsite.
Countdown 5 4 3 2 Stop, get the volunteers to place eggs under their chins. Their hands must remain behind their backs.
Countdown 5 4 3 2 1 Stop, place another egg between the knees of each person
5 4 3 2 1 GO!

Special notes

Expect lots of broken eggs.
Encourage the audience to applaud and encourage the volunteers.

EGG ABUSE

58

![eye]	![wheelchair]	![active]
√	X	√

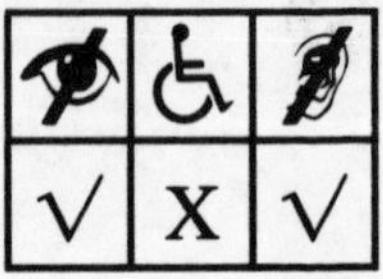

Uptights

Numbers

3, or more

Equipment

Per person:
A pair of tights in the packet.
A blindfold.
A pair of gardening gloves (need to be heavy-duty gloves).

Details

Sit the volunteers on chairs facing the audience. Explain that this is a race to put on the tights over their trousers.
Count down to go — 5 4 3 2 1 Stop, give out the gloves.
Count down, 5 4 3 2 1 Stop, place on the blindfold.
Count down to GO.

Special notes

A great game!
The volunteers can't feel the tights through the gloves or see.
It is funny just to see them wrestling with the basics.
Also funny when eventually they pull the tights over the trousers.
Expect damaged tights!

The Secret Of
My Success

EGG WRESTLING

👁	♿	⚡
√	X	√

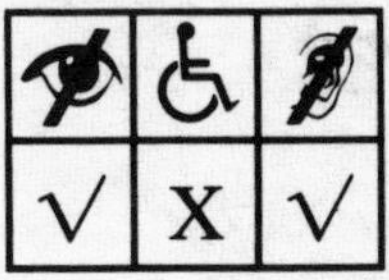

Egg Wrestling

Numbers

2, or more in equal numbers

Equipment

2 eggs per person

Details

Get the volunteers to place an egg under each armpit.
Get the two contestants to face each other and clasp hands.
The aim is to push each other backwards without breaking the eggs.

Special notes

Expect lots of broken eggs.
Better with 3 or 4 couples.
Good for the outdoors in swimwear.

Next time use deodorant CREEP!

60

?	X	√

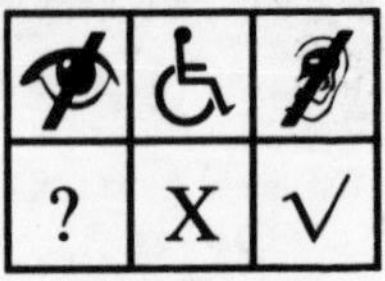

Wine Making

Numbers

3 *volunteers*

Equipment

3 bunches of grapes
3 large plastic bowls (washing-up bowls)
3 sieves and jugs
3 large clear plastic cups

Details

Introduce this as a game needing strength and energy.
The volunteers face the audience, roll up their trousers and remove their foot gear.
They are then instructed to tread the grapes, during the playing of a pop record, and make wine.
At the end, the mixture is sieved and each one measured.
The loser, or better, all three have to drink the wine.

Special notes

Wonderful game for the audience!
A good enthusiastic crowd will encourage this game to a good conclusion.
It is very important that *volunteers* are recruited.

And the first prize
in our youth club
festival is lot number
one . . .

10P FUNNEL

61

👁	♿	🏃
√	X	√

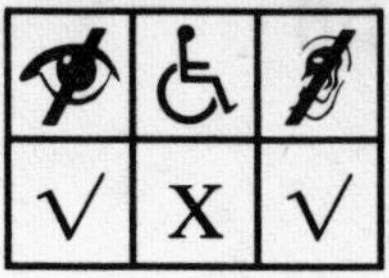

10p Funnel

Numbers

2 or 3 volunteers

Equipment

Per person:
1 funnel
1 10p piece
1 jug of water

Details

Keep the water hidden.
Volunteers face the audience, standing up with their heads back.
A 10p piece is placed on their foreheads.
The aim is to get the 10p into the funnel, which is placed down the trousers/waistband.
The attempts are encouraged in unison.
Count down 5 4 3 2 1 Go.
After two attempts, count down 5 4 etc.
(meanwhile three volunteers creep up behind and just before 'go' they empty the jug of water down the funnel, into the trousers.)

Special notes

Keep the water well hidden.

*If you have no water,
here are some very
interesting alternatives:* The Ice-cubes

The Snake The Ferret

?	?	?

62

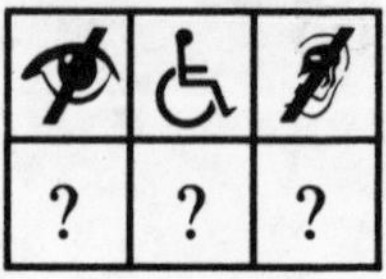

Gargle Queen

Numbers

6 people

Equipment

A cup of water each.

Details

Test everyone can gargle — it's a good laugh to start with.
Each person takes their turn gargling a part of the song, e.g:

1. God save our Gracious Queen
2. Long live our . . .
3. etc. . . .

Special notes

A microphone amplifies the gargle and adds to the fun.

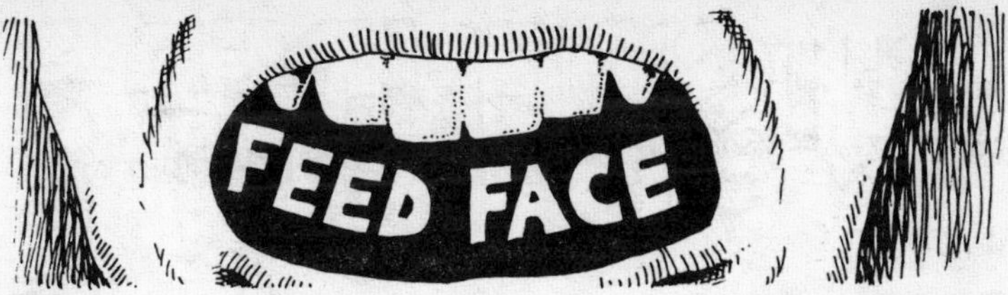

63

👁	♿	🏃
?	X	√

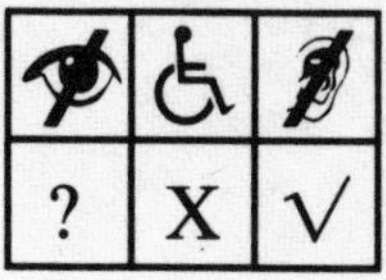

Feed Face

Numbers

2, or more teams of 10

Equipment

For each team:
1 carrier bag,
1 lemon, apple, banana, lollipop,
 jellybaby, onion, choc-bar, carrot,
 can of lemonade and tomato.
2 cream crackers.

Details

This is a race up and down the hill or field.
Run one at a time.
Take first item from the carrier bag.
Run back.
Face audience.
Eat the object.
Next one goes etc.

Special notes

Keep the 'objects' hidden until the hand goes in and selects quickly.

Just make sure
its the onion
that you get.
≈ KISS KISS ≈

SUSPENDERS

64

√	X	√

Suspenders

Numbers

3 couples

Equipment

Suspender belt.
Bra (extra large and filled a little with sewed in bean bags). Stockings (pulled over the trousers). Umbrella. Theatrical make-up. Frop flippers. 3 wigs.

Details

The aim of this game is to make-up a face, with big red lips, white face, blue eyes etc.
Run for equipment one at a time. Run back and the girl fits it on properly.
The winner is first one fully dressed.

Special notes

Team members needed at end of tent to give out equipment in sequence and to tell them to take it back to partner.

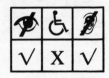

Beware of love-sick frogs

65

Visually impaired	Wheelchair	Hearing impaired
√	?	√

After Eight Mints

Numbers

Teams of 6 to 10

Equipment

One After Eight Mint per person.

Details

On the word 'go' the volunteers have to eat the mint and turn the packet inside out without tearing it.

Special notes

Give everyone present a mint and let them all have a go.

You may wish to practice this game – once a week

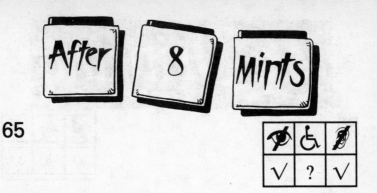

Coke Drinking Contest

66

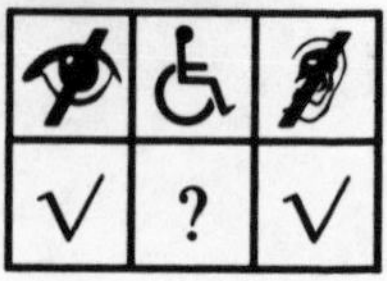
√
?
√

Coke Drinking Contest

Numbers

6 volunteers

Equipment

One can of coke or similar for each contestant. The volunteers must be wearing socks.

Details

Ask for volunteers.
Get them all lined up facing the audience.
Say you will count down 5 4 3 2 1 and on 'go' they drink.
Say 5 4 3 2 Stop.
Ask them to remove one sock and place it over the top of the canned drink.
Say 5 4 3 2 Stop.
Get the volunteers to swop cans with a neighbour.
Say 5 4 3 2 1 GO.
The contestants drink!

Special notes

This is a good audience game. *They* love it.
Use this game in an atmosphere of total abandon.

I'm sorry Zola, you can't play

67

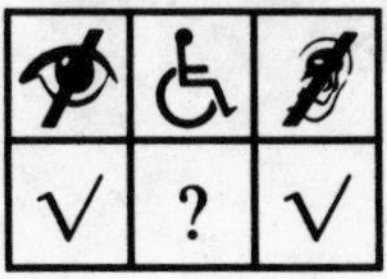

Marathon Gargle

Numbers

6 or more

Equipment

Plastic cups of water.

Details

The participants face the audience.
One cup of water for each person.
The longest gargle wins.

Special notes

You can time each one individually or all participants together.
A microphone amplifies the gargle really well — it adds to the fun.
The participants create the fun in this one.

68

👁	♿	🌿
✓	?	✓

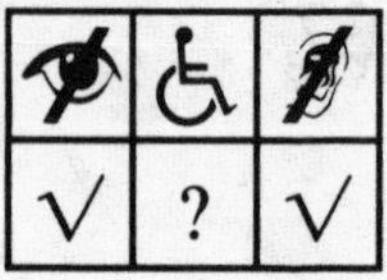

Porcupine Pass

Numbers

A team of 5 – 10 or two teams

Equipment

Toothpicks or cocktails sticks.
Marshmallows (the largest you can buy).

Details

Each person places a toothpick in their mouth.
The first one sticks the marshmallow on to the pick.
Then pass down the marshmallow leaving the toothpick in.
This needs to be done gently as the marshmallow soon develops into a porcupine.

Special notes

Everyone present can play this game if you have one toothpick for everyone and one marshmallow per group.

How do I explain to her mother she swallowed a marshmallow?

69

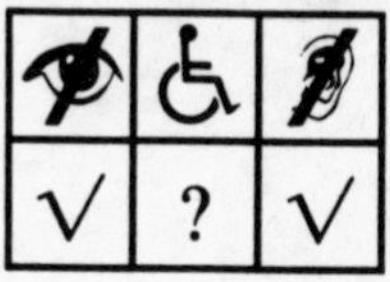

Bubble Yum

Numbers

6 – 10

Equipment

Wrapped bubble gum.

Details

Give each person a piece of wrapped bubble gum.
On a signal they must put the gum into their mouths, wrapper and all, and unwrap the gum in their mouths.
They spit the paper out, chew the gum and blow a bubble.
First one to get a bubble wins.

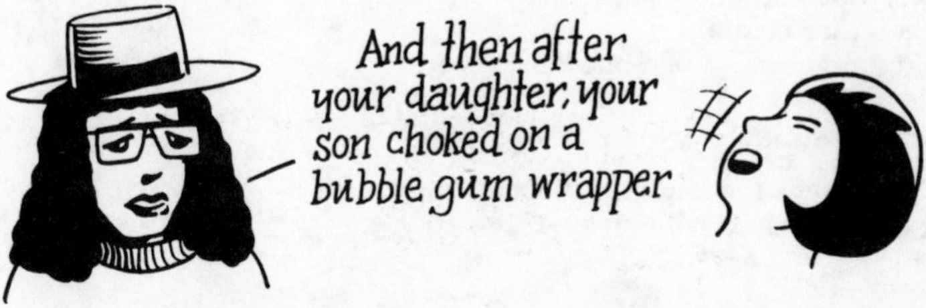

And then after your daughter, your son choked on a bubble gum wrapper

3z CHAIN

70

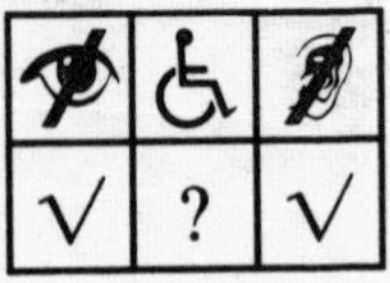

3z Chain

Numbers

3, or multiples of 3

Equipment

Per 3 participants:
Masking tape.
3 tooth brushes.
1 tube toothpaste.

Details

Tape their hands together.
Give tasks:
Clean teeth with toothpaste and brushes.
Untie and then tie all the laces in their shoes.
Blow their noses.
Somersault.
Go and buy a doughnut and eat it (or anything else from a local shop).
Comb hair.
Eat an ice cream.
Eat 3 crackers — one bite each.

Special notes

The game is fun and not competitive.
It can be played with many or few.

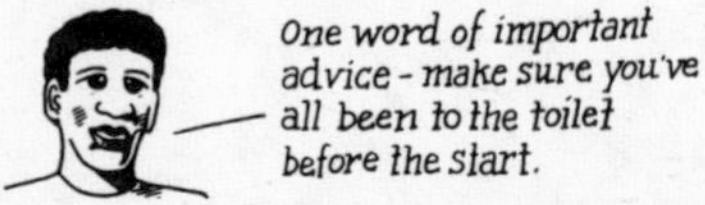

One word of important advice - make sure you've all been to the toilet before the start.

71

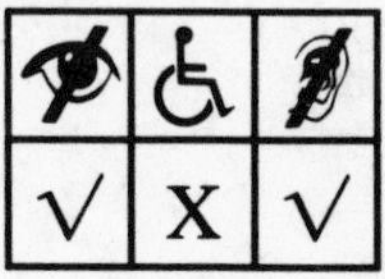

Foot Sign

Numbers

6–10 people, or everyone present

Equipment

Biro pens or felt tip pens.

Details

Say you will count down 5 4 3 2 1 Go.
Ask them to collect signatures from as many people as they can in 3 minutes.
Say 5 4 3 2 1 STOP – on your bare feet! Take your shoes and socks off. 5 4 3 2 1 Go!

Special notes

As with all games, the build-up and the unexpected help to create the excitement. It is good to play this game for the duration of one record which brings the game to an end naturally.
It is best if everyone is a winner, rather than spending time selecting one winner. Fun is the object!

72

√	X	√

Water Feet

Numbers

3 teams of about 10 people
(a minimum of 2 groups of 5)

Equipment

2 bowls ¾ full of water. (4 or 5 litre ice cream containers are ideal.)

Details

The teams sit in a circle, then lie on their backs with their feet up in the centre of the circle.
The helpers balance the water bowl on the feet of the group members.
The aim is for all group members to remove their shoes without spilling water.

Special notes

Really good game, particularly for the audience!
Some groups spill the water immediately.
Other groups do it well, but usually end up with wet legs.
Expect a wet floor.

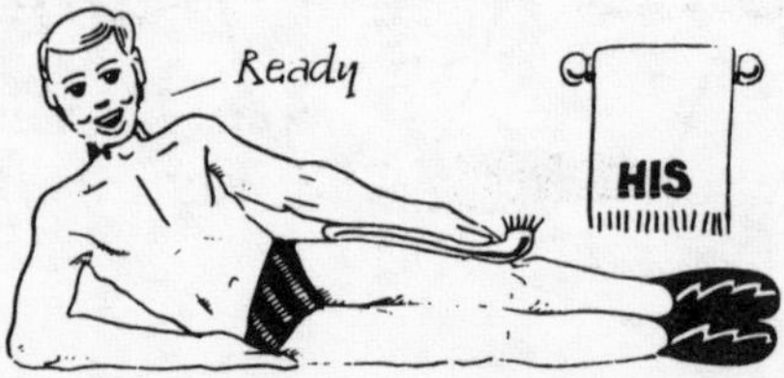

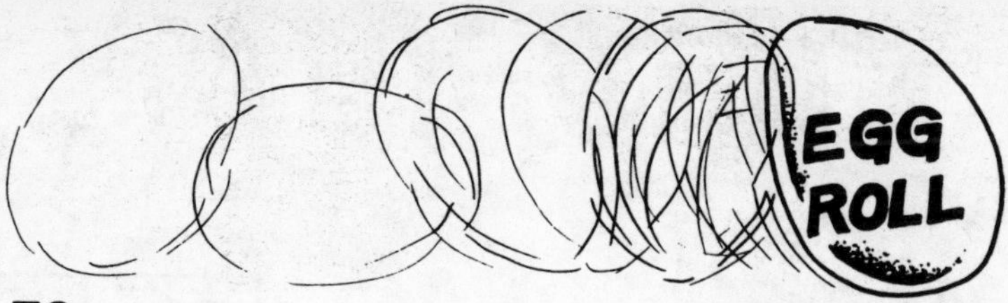

73

√	X	√

Egg Roll

Numbers

2 or 3 (or could be team race)

Equipment

One fresh egg each.

Details

Push an egg around the hall or marquee pole with the nose, racing against the opposing team.
If the egg breaks start again.

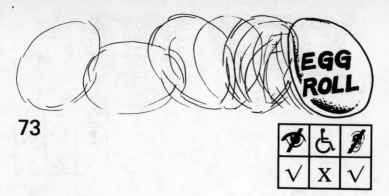

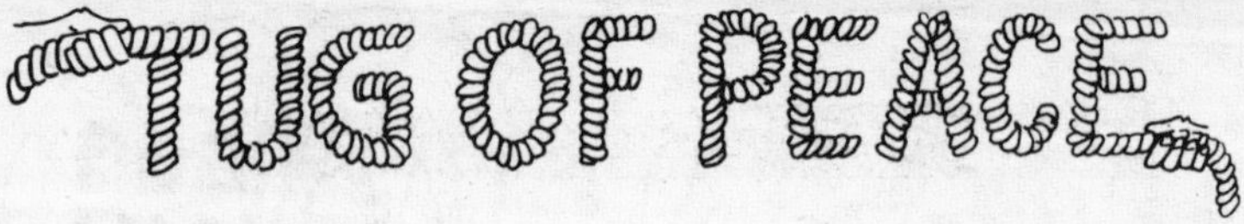

74

√	X	√

Tug of Peace

Numbers

Lots of small groups of 6–10

Equipment

Skipping ropes — enough for all the groups.

Details

Give each group a rope.
Begin in seated position.
Get them to form a letter or shape and stand up using tension or pull to form shape.
Ideas: Triangle/square/circle.

Special notes

The aim is co-operation — not competition.

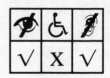

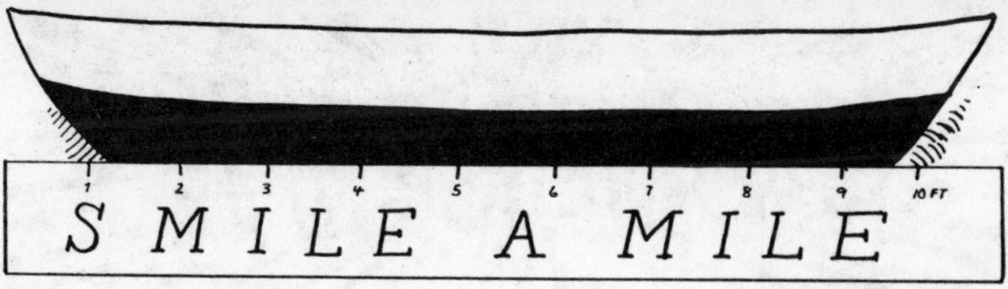

75

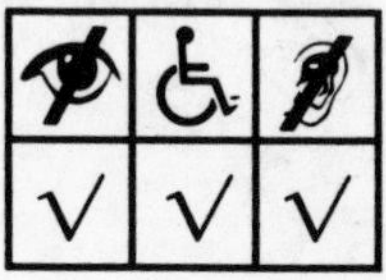

Smile a Mile

Numbers

5–10

Equipment

Ruler

Details

The aim is to find the widest smile.
Line up the group facing the audience, measure each mouth (note the distance on paper).
The widest smile is applauded and asked to demonstrate.

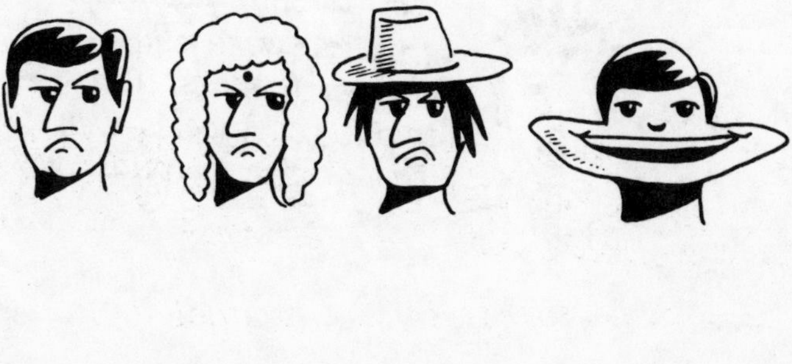

76

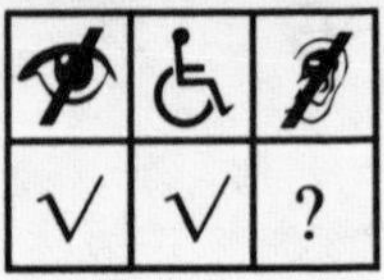

Suddenly

Numbers

5–10

Equipment

None

Details

Have a team in line. One starts a story . . . 'I walked to Greenbelt and I bumped into this beautiful blonde girl and *suddenly* . . .' After each '*suddenly*' the next person takes the story on. Keep going as long as is necessary.

... of course, my holidays this year were jolly well cheaper than last years trip to Los Angeles, even though the cooking....

ELECTRIC CHAIR

| ✓ | X | ✓ |

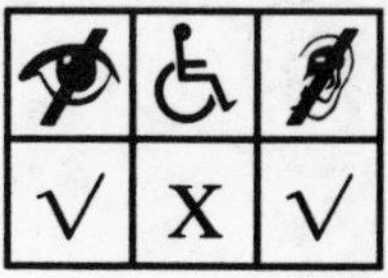

Electric Chair

Numbers

10–15

Equipment

None

Details

Get everyone to form a circle and hold hands (8–15 group size).
One person drops out and kneels.
The group try to get each other to the 'chair' — that person then drops out and the circle carries on.
This can also be played with the backs to centre of the circle.

Not a game to be played at crabs parties

78

√	X	√

Team Roll

Numbers

2 teams of 6–10, or everyone present

Equipment

None

Details

2 teams lie down in line side by side, face down.
'Go' – the first one rolls over the team to the back, then the next until all have rolled upon everyone.

Special notes

This is a wonderful game for a crowded marquee at a summer camp or festival, in an environment where fun takes priority over dust and sweat!
Not so appropriate for guests at a wedding reception.

I lost more weight playing this, than through drinking Bai-Lin tea.
ADVERTISMENT

ONE MINUTE SHOWER

79

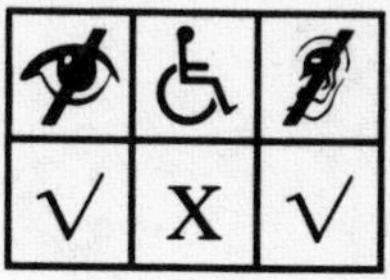

One Minute Shower

Numbers

Minimum 6

Equipment

Shower or a bucket with holes.
Ample supply of water.

Details

Challenge everyone to tackle this record breaking attempt.
Pour some water into the bucket. On the word 'go', one at a time, the group run under the shower as quickly as possible. Someone count the number of times through the shower — keep the time to one minute.

Special notes

Especially good if someone slips!
Repeat again later to try to break the record.
Try two teams — 10 boys versus 10 girls.
See how many can go through in a minute — around and around again.

80

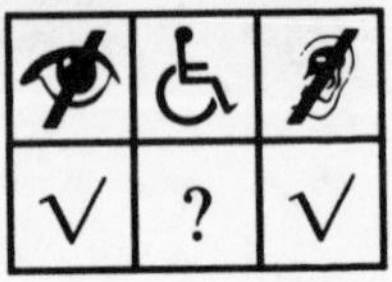

Li-Lo

Numbers

15 plus

Equipment

One li-lo (a single person air bed).

Details

Everyone lies down on their backs alternating head to feet close together.
The li-lo is placed on the raised hands at one end of the row.
The end person dives on and hangs on for dear life as the li-lo is passed along on a row of hands.
The next person then takes a ride.

Special notes

This can be played in a circle with a never ending ride!
Needs a person responsible for safety at the ends to catch the rider.

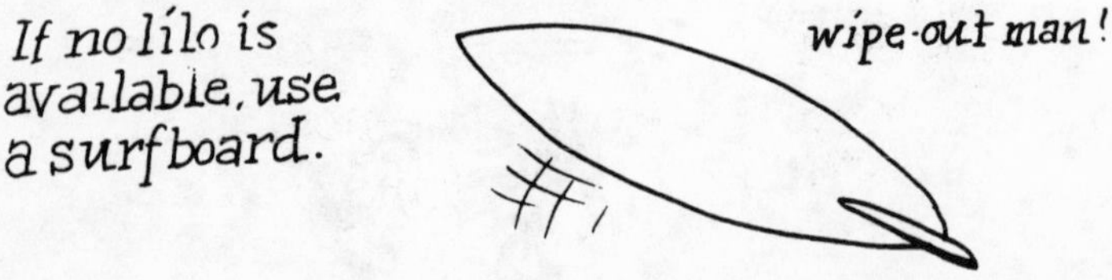

If no lilo is available, use a surfboard.
wipe-out man!

RUDOLPH

81

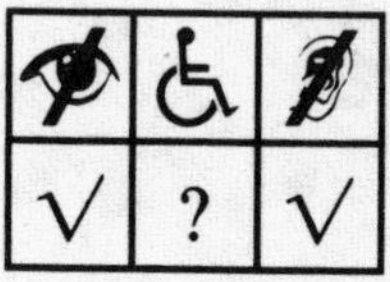

Rudolph

Numbers

2 teams of equal numbers

Equipment

2 tubes of cheap lipstick

Details

Line up two teams.
Deposit a large amount of lipstick all over the first volunteer's NOSE.
On the word 'go' the aim is to pass the red lipstick down the line by rubbing noses to see which team can have a 'Rudolph' at the other end of line.

Special notes

With a really friendly group alternate boy/girl.
May wish to apply lipstick to the lips and pass a kiss down the line!

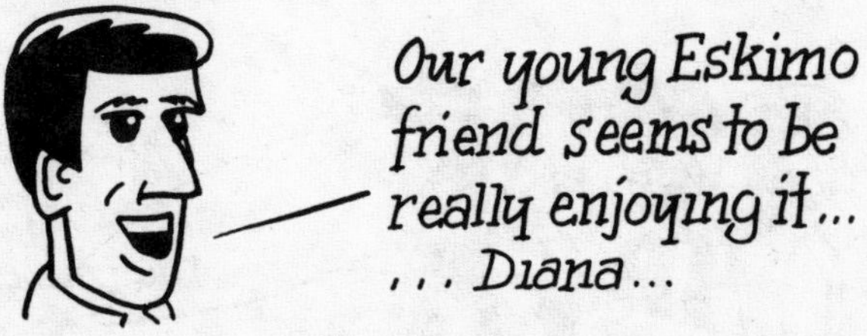

Our young Eskimo friend seems to be really enjoying it...
... Diana...

SKIP TO THE LOO

82

👁	♿	🪢
√	X	√

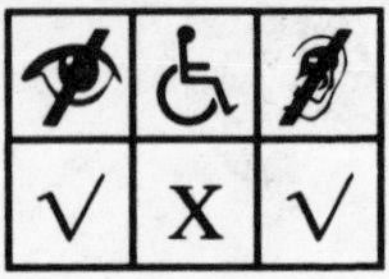

Skip to the Loo

Numbers

Groups of approximately 6

Equipment

Skipping ropes for every group (the thicker climbing rope is best).

Details

Get everyone in groups of 6 with a rope each. Get them to stand close together and tie the rope around themselves. This is usually an enjoyable part of the game. On the word 'go' all the groups have to run along the field/hall around a suitable marker (e.g. a toilet seat???).

Special notes

The teams usually try to run too fast and fall over. Chaos ensues with much laughter. If appropriate, it is better for everyone to remove their shoes.

Combine this with the game 'One Minute Shower' and that really speeds up the game.

" The bound
leading
the bound "

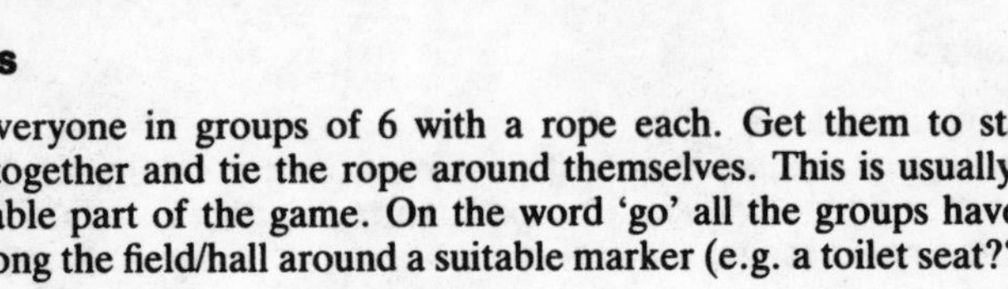

GROUPWORK
GAMES

Section Four
Groupwork Games

Gut Games

Introduction
There are different *Gut Games* here. Gut Games are games that create feelings, so choose ones that are suitable for each situation. In Gut Games groups share, individuals interact and contribute to each other's learning. Social skills are learned which help us cope in our society. Political skills are learned which change attitudes and hopefully result in social *action*. Mistakes are made, but in a secure environment, which is Good News for both individuals and the whole group. It's the pressure-cooker theory. Create an experience, a real experience, in an atmosphere of learning and we learn quickly in a safe environment. These experiences can be life changing.

Experiential Gut Games
Certain games are definitely experiential. (A structured experience that creates real feelings which needs some follow up e.g. discussion or analysis.) Here is a suggested process.

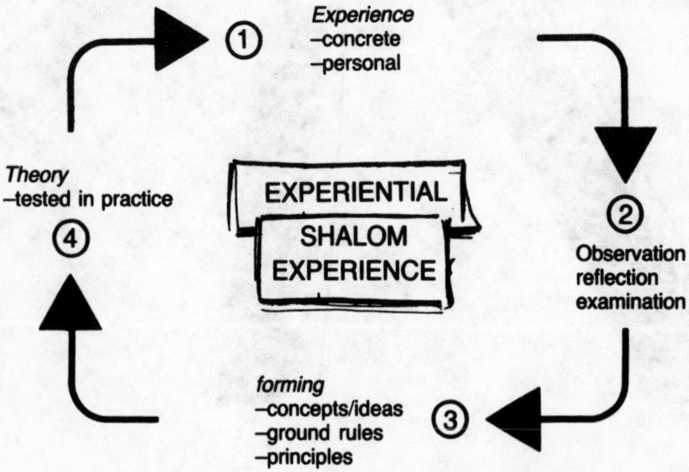

The experience

1. **Structure** the game you are playing. Experience it, feel it but *don't* go on to the next game just for the fun of it. Continue through this process with all your games.
2. The **Reflection** stage is next. Any game/structured experience/exercise that has created some feeling can be reflected upon.

   The process of many of the Participation Games and Crazy Games in Sections two and three can be examined and used for growth purposes, by questioning each other and through discussion.
3. The **(re) Forming** of principles during and following real experiences happens whether we structure it or not. As with the values we adopt in our childhood, we learn mainly by absorption; like water into a sponge, rather than from a list of principles.

   We can, however, heighten learning by sharing experiences at this stage and outlining principles for action in our lives.
4. **Theory Testing** to check it out. Monitoring, Application, and Theory to practice is the last step in this continuous cycle. This phase is a joy to experience in the life of an ongoing group. We can *see growth*, however small, as members of the group live their experience out in their daily lives.

Sensitivity

Some games need special leadership skills. It is advisable *not* to attempt a game if you don't feel competent.

This special sensitivity is required because some games disturb feelings and can damage relationships and leave individuals hurt. We must never press people into participating in any activity that they do not wish to join in.

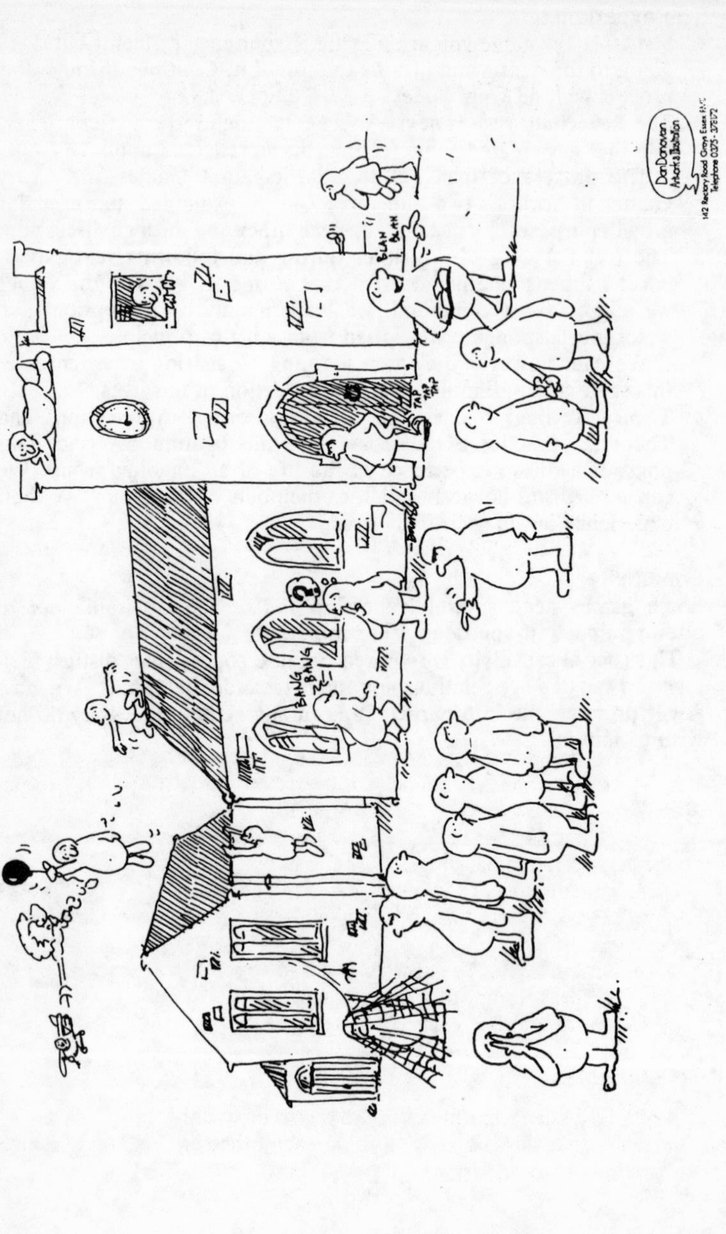
BANG BANG
TAP TAP TAP
BLAH BLAH
Dan Donovan
Artwork & Illustration
142 Rectory Road Grays Essex

83

Non-sexist Blob Church

Numbers

Best in small groups of 6–10 (maximum)
(If there are more than 10 people present divide into groups)

Equipment

Copy of Blob Church.
Pen or pencil.

Details

The aim of this game is to encourage sharing and listening.

a. Ask each person to think of a group that they belong to: Church group, friendship group, school, work, golf club.

b. Ask them to choose which 'blob' they identify with in the context of that group (as in 'a' above).

c. Ask them to share in their group which blob they identify with and why. Ask the group to listen and ask questions if they don't understand.

d. Ask members of the groups to share which blob they would like to be — or draw in another blob figure!

e. Go on to another group activity.

Special notes

Alternative. Ask group members to share in two/threes.
Emphasise that this is a game to help each other disclose real feelings and the aim is to *understand* not condemn.

84

Hobby

Numbers

Everybody (ideal in groups of 6–10)

Equipment

None

Details

Ask everyone in turn to describe their favourite hobby non-verbally. When guessed it is the next person's turn. It may be good in your context to get one person (perhaps the leader!) up front to demonstrate his/her hobby.

OBJECT

85

Object

Numbers

Everybody (buzzing in 2/3s)

Equipment

None

Details

Choose any item in your possession.
Spend one minute in silence thinking about it.
Share with the person next to you all about it.
It could be a lipstick, hanky, coin, pen, creditcard, wallet, a note, photograph, car key, house key, or comb etc.

Special notes

It is surprising and revealing that a simple game like this can be so satisfying.
Group workers could join in too!

86

Non-sexist Blob Tree

Numbers

Best in small groups (6–10) or in twos or threes

Equipment

A copy of 'The Tree' for each member.
A pen or pencil each.

Details

Distribute copies of 'The Tree' around the group.
Ask the members to choose a group that they belong to: the office, the factory, sports team, church group, Youth Club group — any group.
Then ask the members to choose one 'blob' that they identify with in the context of that group.
Ask the members to share with the group (or in twos or threes) which blob they are and why they selected this one.

Special notes

This is an ideal 'starter' for a group/fellowship session or weekend house party.
The aim is to encourage self revelation — knowing one self.
The game brings out 'feelings', so sensitivity is needed.

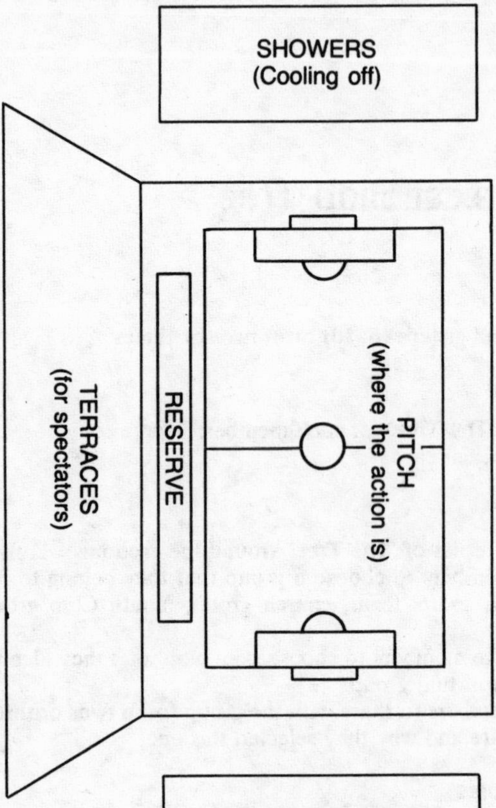
SHOWERS
(Cooling off)
TERRACES
(for spectators)
RESERVE
PITCH
(where the action is)
CHANGING ROOM
(getting in shape)

87

God's Football Pitch

Numbers

Suitable for small or large groups; or sharing in twos or threes

Equipment

Copies of the pitch for everyone or a very large copy of the pitch that all can see.

Details

This is a particularly effective method of helping people to know where they are in relationship to God.

The question is: Where are you on the pitch? Where are you in relationship to God?
— are you on the *terraces*, just a spectator?
— are you in the *changing rooms* getting ready for action?
— are you perhaps even closer to God, on the *reserve bench*?
— or are you a Christian, on *the pitch* — where the action is? Others may place themselves in *the showers* — cooling off from the action of being a Christian. Some youth workers have placed themselves here — feeling tired, battered, soiled and needing refreshment before returning to the pitch.

In a youth club, for instance, this pitch has been used to get kids to think and publicly declare where they are. I always remember Ingrid, a beautiful black girl, walking from the disco area across the social area to place herself on the terraces. Others have said, 'I'm in the pub on the corner of the next street!' or, 'I'm on the terraces with my back to the pitch!' (That says a lot, doesn't it?) Bones, an eighteen-year-old boy, placed himself on the terraces, but a week later in the midst of a chat pointed out that he had moved to the changing rooms — getting ready!

This device is used a lot in youth clubs to make it easier to talk about Christian things. Kids easily respond or bring up the subject without any feeling of threat. Among Christians it is also a very useful device for cultivating spiritual self-disclosure.

Youth workers can be asked: 'Where are you on the pitch at the moment?' 'I'm on the pitch — the touch line, but no one is passing me the ball', said a keen Christian. What does that say? Here are other responses I've heard during the years:

'I'm on the pitch, but lying on a stretcher.'

'I'm on the pitch, but with shins bleeding, playing defence all the time.'

'I'm scoring goals!'

'Mid-field distributing the ball and keeping abreast of the game.'

'I'm dirty, knackered, sweaty — but I'm on the pitch.'

In the *Rolling Magazine* Fun Tent that I head up at Greenbelt Christian Arts Festival every year, 'The Pitch' is used effectively to cultivate sharing in small groups as well as to challenge the known Christian celebrities and artistes. Where are you on God's pitch?

88

Bio

Numbers

Everybody (maximum 10 per group)

Equipment

A file card per person.
Pen/pencil per person.

Details

Give out the file cards and pencils to every person present.
Ask them to do an instant autobiography.
No names on the cards.
Collect and shuffle the cards.
Distribute them and ask each group member in turn to read out the details.
Group members then have to guess who it is.

Special notes

Ideas: I was born . . .
my favourite pop star . . .
my favourite meal . . .
my favourite car . . .
my favourite TV soap . . .
I cry when . . .
I am angry when . . .
etc.

If there is any chance of a person not being able to read, have only one person to read out the cards.

FEELING FACES

what do you feel when....

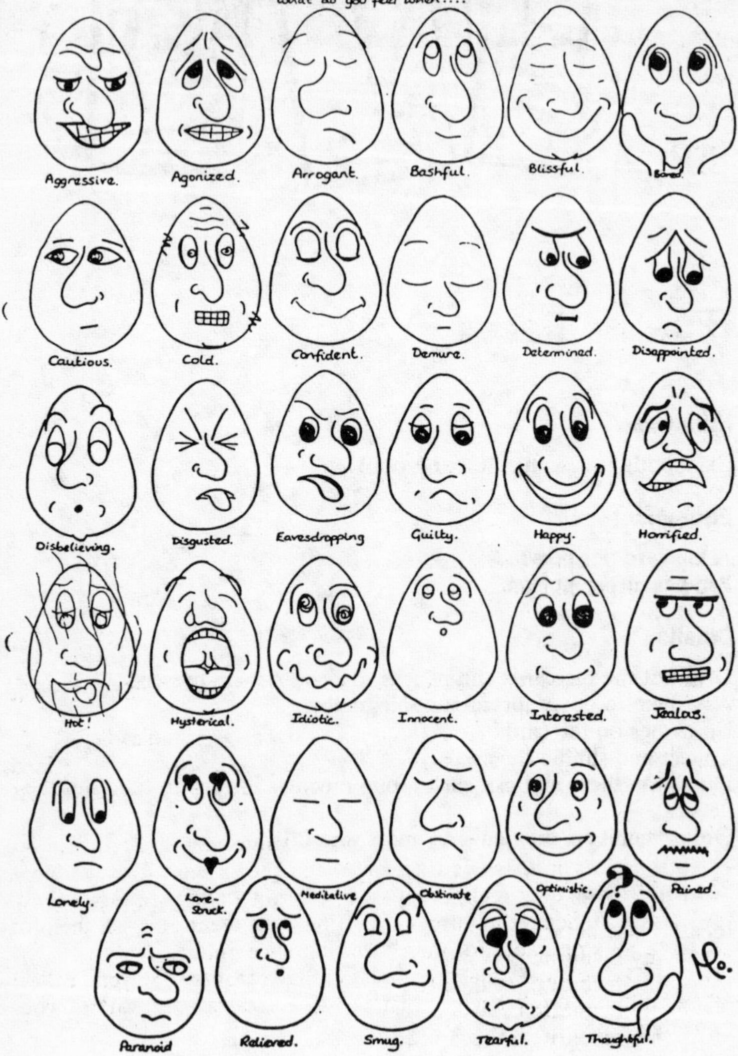

FEELING FACES

89

Feeling Faces

Numbers

Small groups (6–10) or twos/threes

Equipment

Copies of Feeling Faces for everyone.
A pen or pencil each.

Details

The *Aim* of this exercise is to cultivate openness and honesty through self revelation of the innermost feelings.
Levelling with each other with view to sharing joys and sadness.
Levelling with others can cultivate levelling with Jesus who walked the earth as a man of feeling, a man of sorrows who knew the desert experience.
(i) At the very beginning of the session before any other announcements, notices or activities ask everyone to keep a short time of silence and note how they feel. Emphasise it is not bodily feelings ('tired' 'sore throat' 'headache' 'broken leg') but 'gut feelings'. Ask them to make a note on paper for their own reference only.
(ii) Introduce the normal group session. Give notices, prayers, collect subscriptions, drink tea — whatever is normal at the start of your meeting.

(iii) Divide members into groups of 6–10 and ask them to sit in a circle.
(iv) Pass out copies of 'Feeling Faces' and ask the members of the group to share with one other person next to them, or in threes. Ask them to select a 'face' that is nearest their feelings at this moment. There may be embarrassed laughter. Gently press them to be open and truthful even if it is revealing!
(v) Ask them to share again. This time the feelings that they noted at the beginning of the meeting/session.
Ask them to share and then compare.
(vi) After some time of discussion in twos or threes open up the discussion to a wider group. Ask the group to discuss the reasons *why* their feelings have changed. What activities have touched their feelings.

Discussion Points.
1. 'The longest journey is the journey inward.' Dag Hammarskjold.
2. 'To know people well is to know their tragedy. It's usually the thing most people's lives are built around. We cry into the night and there is no reply.' Bertrand Russell.
3. 'After Jesus said this, he went off and hid himself from them. Even though he had performed all these miracles in their presence, they did not believe in him . . .' Bible (John 12:36–37).

Levelling like this can provide a refreshing climate for sharing faith in life's journey together.

90

Me Circle

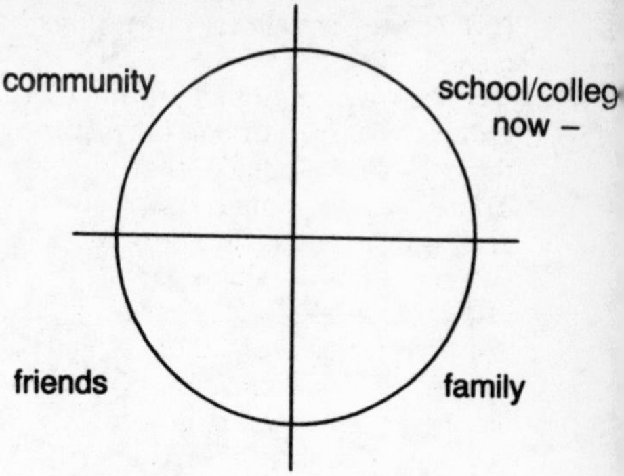

Numbers

6–8 people

Equipment

Pen and paper each.

Details

Draw very large circle, similar to the one illustrated, or provide individuals with a smaller version each. Provide a pen or pencil for each participant.
Explain

(i) Write your own name in the centre of the circle.
(ii) Write in another name of a person whom you feel most warmth from/to.
(iii) Place one name in each section relating them all in distances from yourself.
(iv) Write in all members of your family or those who you live with.
(v) Get into groups of two or threes and have them share their diagram.
(vi) Bring back the group together and encourage discussion. Affirm and be sensitive as it could create extra feelings.
(vii) Ask individual to place God on the diagram not where they think. He should be but where he honestly *is* in 'warmth' terms.
(viii) Discuss and share.

Special notes

Explain that this game is no judgment on people who we know and have as friends but more of a current feelings analysis.
Expect lots of questions.

I RAN THE WORLD
by IAN LONG
110 BIRMINGHAM RD
ALDRIDGE, WALSALL

91

The Preacher

Numbers

Everyone in groups of 6–10

Equipment

A copy of *The Preacher* each, or one very large one for all to see.

Details

Everyone belongs to a group.
Church, School, Office, Friendship Group, Club, Golf Club, College, Family Group etc.
Divide each group into 'threes'.
Ask them to choose a group that they belong to (as above).
Ask then to select a 'Blob Figure' which they identify with.
Share with the other two people:
which blob? why this one?

Special notes

Many variations are possible.
Be very sensitive to those who may feel 'friendless'

92

One Lie

Numbers

Groups, large or small

Equipment

Pen and paper each.

Details

The *aim* is to stimulate sharing with increasing openness.
Ask everyone to answer all the questions but one must be a lie.
This could take a whole evening.

Method One
Get all assembled into groups of three. Decide if it is best to mix them up or group with near neighbours.
Read phase one questions out and have all participants note their answers on a piece of paper. Then ask them to tell one as a lie when they share in groups of three. The other members of the group then have to guess which is the lie (then they say what the truth is!).
Follow with the questions for Phase Two.

Method Two
Use with all the group together. This needs lively leadership. It is ideal at the start of a weekend or houseparty etc. and will create lots of shared humour and cohesiveness.
Read out phase one and get them to note their answers quickly.
Then go around the room asking for a public sharing of the answers (and the lie). Get the whole group to vote which is 'the lie'. Then ask for the truthful revelation.
Follow with the questions for Phase Two.

Note. There will be much humour and jesting during this game — but *also* lots of meaningful sharing that is dynamic for a group and a *real* sharing of faith.

THE QUESTIONS

Phase One

1. What is your favourite meal?
2. What is your favourite room at home?
3. Who is your favourite singer?
4. When you get in the bath, which 'bit' do you wash first?
5. What makes you feel most angry?

Phase Two

1. Who would you like to be stuck in a lift with?
2. If you could, which bit of your body would you swop?
3. What colour is Monday to you?
4. In what situation do you feel most vulnerable or uneasy?
5. At what time of your life did God become a source of warmth?

GUT
GAME
POEMS

Gut Game Poems — Introduction

Numbers

Best in small groups of 6–10

Equipment

A copy of the poem.
A clear prepared reader!

Details

I have a friend called Howard who is a member of our 'Gut Games' team who hit a House Party or Festival occasionally. He writes incredible poems that amuse and entertain. Others strike deeply into our thought processes and our spirituality. A number suitable for group use are enclosed in this section.

Leaders' notes

How to use this section

1. Types of use.
(*a*) a whole evening of poems and discussion.
(*b*) use one as group de-froster before the activities.
(*c*) use one as a concluding item following other activities.
2. (*a*) Have the poem read by someone who has prepared and can competently communicate or
(*b*) hand out a copy to each group member.
3. Discussion. Ask everyone's view leaving the most talkative ones to the last.

Don't crush anyone. Acknowledge and affirm each person as you ask for their comment. Open up to a discussion only when everyone has had an initial comment.

Allow individuals to learn from each other. Don't end by telling them the real answer — you ain't got it!

The Magnificent Ruin

Man is so great
He can fly with the birds
He can swim with the fish
He can even break out of the sky
And touch the moon.
Man can produce twice as much food as he needs
Yet he still hungers somewhere.
Man cares so much about new and old life
Yet he still kills millions in wars.
Man talks so much about love
Yet still 1 in 3 marriages don't end up so loving.
Man can spend £4m on a spaceman's back pack
Yet he can still be poor with no money to feed himself.
Could God really have intended us
To spend so much on weapons
That by a few weeks abstinence
The whole world's food, housing and health problem
Would be solved?
Whatever man is
He is not what he was meant to be.

Think on these things:
What must God think of what we the western world spends its money on? Can the spending on nuclear weapons and its threat ever be right?

Howard Searle

Let's Pretend

Let's pretend
Let's pretend we're friends
Without having to go to any trouble
Like getting to know each other.

Let's pretend
Let's pretend we're mates
That we've shared our experiences
When we've only been drinking together.

Let's pretend
Let's pretend we're close
Though we only want to joke and laugh
Never want to listen or cry.

Let's pretend about friendship
That we can take it automatically
Without ever having to give or try.

Let's pretend
We're friends.

Think on these things:
How real are our friendships? Can we rely and be relied upon?

Howard Searle

Good Infection

It's a good infection
Through the whole cross-section
And at close inspection
Seems like nothing's wrong.

It affects black and white
Through the stars and stripes
In the left and the right
Seems it's never gone.

It's always in history
Through to future society
In you and in me
In the words of a song.

What have we done
Put the world on the run
'Cos we're still playing God
Looking after number one.

Think on these things:
If we stopped putting ourselves first, individually and as a nation, then perhaps the world could change and God's kingdom come.

Howard Searle

Someone's Got to Speak for The Child

Mothers screamed, their babies cried
When the soldiers came, their babies died.

If they were under two, they couldn't deny
By Herod's order they had to die.

The swords plunged in, killed life throughout.
The swords plunged in, their blood poured out.

They murdered babies like we still do
We steal life, it could have been you.

I am the child that you won't know
You want me gone so I won't grow.

No crime have I done, to deserve such fate
Conceived out of passion, aborted by hate.

The knife plunged in, sliced through my bones
The knives plunge in, do you hear my groans.

They cut me up and that was it
Then they sucked me out bit by bit.

They reassembled me to check nothing was there
In the womb of the mother I thought would have cared.

A severed head, a product of sin
In a black plastic bag, laid to rest in a bin.

There I lay with countless others
Just one day's work from life-saving doctors.

Think on these things:
If people's and society's attitudes changed towards single mothers and pregnancies out of marriage, being less destructive socially and financially, then perhaps there would be no need for abortions.

Life-Aid

Why is it always kidney machines and hospitals
or some other helpful yet vital institution
That we raise money for?
Don't the army or navy need anything?
When did you last hear of a charity fun-run
In aid of a heat-seeking ballistic missile?
Perhaps it's true then
The armed forces don't need anything
But it's also true then
That hospitals and other life-saving places
Aren't given anywhere enough in the first place
By our leaders who have the power to give away our money.
'It's the kidney machines that pay for rockets and guns.'

Think on these things:
How should we care about what the government does with our nation's money?
'Give to Caesar what is Caesar's, and to God what is God's.' Luke 20:25.

Howard Searle

Weather Report

'Box office records go'
In major headlines
'£1m taken in 3 days'
In large black print
'Rambo's the biggest movie ever'
Spread over most of the page.
'Walk out strike fails'
In minor headlines
'South African miners against inhuman apartheid'
In small faint print
'Bosses threatened sack and eviction from lodgings'
In the bottom corner of the page.
So what is more important?

Sun sun go away
And don't come back another day.

Think on these things!
How are the attitudes of people in our society influenced by what newspapers print? What sort of newspaper should we read? Are we aware of what happens in this world we live in?

Howard Searle

Building Bridges Not Fences

Man in authority uniform kicks hell out of a black
In another country a person turns their back.
Man in balaclava pays wrong back with wrong
Across the nearby border they're already making bombs.
Man on picket line duty hurls his 'mate' a brick
Behind the lines young boy blue gives another kick.
Man in pin-stripe suit tells a 'little' white lie
In secret rooms the deals are made no one answers why.
Man who thinks R2 D2 tries to start star wars
The way to peace is more weapons not justice for the poor.
Man in the east is gaoled for saying what he's thinking
In South American stadiums prison chains are secretly clinking.
Man in whole wide world acts out of his senses
We should be building bridges, so why are there all these fences.

Think on these things:
How much of the world's conflict is due to political and religious beliefs where people accept nothing but their own beliefs? Do we listen to people who we disagree with? How can we 'build bridges'? What did Jesus say about enemies?

Howard Searle

Church Not Made By Hands

Churches which are built
To try and trap God's presence
So that they are in some way holy
Are doomed to failure.
They may have been built in 50 years
But they are not really complete.
They could be torn down
And it would not really matter.
For what is really important
Was re-built on the Third day.
Only when God is built
Into individual lives
Will the church become completed.

Think on these things:
What is the attitude of the Church and its massive wealth in land and property to the disadvantaged sections of society?
What should it be?

Howard Searle

Valentine

It's a cardseller's delight
And for the traders a welcome relief
After the new year sales have gone down.
Almost everything you can buy
Is translated as saying 'I love you' —
'Say it with flowers'
'Prove your love with natural fur'
'Put your message in the press'
'Send heart-shaped chocolates to show you care'
Who would have thought that
Nature could realise such a profit
In such a beautiful thing as a rose.
Is love blind
Or are we merely short-sighted?
They say it's about romance
But it's really about money.
Meanwhile the Empire State building
Changes its lights
To flash red and white
Over the city for 2 nights
Is anything left untouched and pure today?

Think on these things:
How far will the business world in our society go to commercialise everything they can from Christmas to Easter and back again?
What should be our attitude to such materialism?
What did Jesus do to the money-changers in the Temple?

Howard Searle

Expensive Love

Love is such an expensive word
Yet it is used so cheaply these days.
Love is such a strong word
Yet used so weakly.
Plastered around the top 40
Packed in bookshops, in porno mags.
It's thought of as corny
That man should love each other
But if we thought of love in its fullness of
Justice, forgiveness, truth,
Love your neighbour as yourself
Would seem more revolutionary.
That's why when properly used
Love is such an expensive word.
Jesus loves us fully
And the amazing thing is
He gives his love to all of us for free.

Think on these things:
What does 'love' mean to us and how should it affect our daily lives and relationships? What did it mean to Jesus?

Howard Searle

Injustice Is a Crime Too

If we truly thought about it
Then if the total violations of law and justice
By government, oppressors, white man,
Were calculated over the years:
Inferior education, poor housing, unemployment,
Inadequate health care, economic slavery, prejudice,
And were compared with the law-breaking of a few riots
Who would the hardened criminal be?
Yet that is no excuse
For the murder of an innocent policeman.

Think on these things:
Why are economic crimes not seen to be as bad as physical crimes?
Would big business lose too much if there were economic justice?
What should the government's and our attitude be to apartheid in South Africa?

Howard Searle

Bottle

I want to catch you in a bottle
And place you on a shelf
To be surrounded in your presence
To remind me of myself.

I want to capture and define you
To look at you from below
So there's nothing left to search for
So there's nothing left to know.

I want to reach out to all of you
So you can fill me from within
But I know it's all so hopeless
When I refuse to let you in.

You're all around you're everywhere
Beyond any dictionary definition
Infinite, soul-searching
Beyond human imagination.

Love which died yet lives again
Love which fuels the sun
Love which gives me all I need
Scorch some fire into this one.

Think on these things:
In what part of our lives can we let God take more control?

Howard Searle

Too Late

When help comes
Know it's too late
To save the dying hundreds
From an empty plate.

It takes a lot to make us cry
Perhaps the death of someone close
Not it seems the death of a nation
For if we really cared
We would really have shared.

When help comes
Know it's still too late
To save the dying thousands
From a hopeless wait.

When we do finally notice
It's because of a TV screen
We only give in the final scene.
For if we really had love
There would surely be more to give.

When help comes
Know it may be too late
To save the dying millions
From all our hate.

We only give when we see the truth
But this truth exists all the time
Pray God he'll somehow stop the dying.
For if we really had no greed
There would surely be no third world need.

Think on these things:
What causes hunger like we have seen in Africa? Has the exploitation by the rest of the world affected this e.g. loan debt financial problems? Why is God blamed when we have the resources to solve the problem? What can we do personally — support overseas development agencies or buy Third World goods directly from them, e.g. Oxfam, without the exploitation?

Violence — A Growth Game

Numbers

Best played in small group(s) of 6–10.
An experienced group worker could handle several small groups in the same hall. One small group is recommended.

Equipment

A large copy of figure 1 (or copy for all participants)-.
A copy of reading 1 on page 148 (*Gutter Feelings*).
A copy of reading 2 on page 169 (*Guardian* 15/2/86).
A copy of reading 3 on page 169 (*Guardian* 2/86).
Copies of the Feeling Faces page 138.
Bible(s).
Pencil and paper.
A large piece of paper.
Felt tip pens.
Two rooms: main room plus one other to enable movement in and out quite quickly and easily.

Introduction for the Leader

1. This has been planned to be a self-contained session.
2. Don't feel restricted by it! Use it, if you wish, straight from the paper, but feel free to adapt and add according to the needs of your group.
3. Add any current news items that are relevant to the subject *and* the group.
4. The main aim is to facilitate participants to think beyond their normal understanding, by an experience-based session. To explore, alongside this, bible passages and the attitudes and values we can learn from them.

Introduction and Ice Breaking Session (*)

This is a light-hearted few minutes to get everyone participating, contributing and relaxed.

(*a*) In twos or threes where they are sitting, the participants are asked to tell their partner *what colour they are!* ('Not your favourite colour, or your skin colour, but what colour that, it seems to you, describes your personality and character.') Feedback is taken in a light-hearted manner, which brings the group together cohesively. Welcome humour and use 'in jokes' to help everyone feel they belong.

(*b*) Next Question to share with partner.
'What colour is God?', same brief as before with feedback as above.

Plan

The idea now is to enable participants to relax even more by knowing what is planned. The session is explained, i.e. the process and the method. It experientially means that:

> Certain activities during the session are structured to create *feelings* in individuals and an atmosphere change in the group. These will enable the group to talk about *actual concrete feelings* rather than mainly concepts/theory.

Use this model to explain what is about to happen in language that your group understands (be aware of the group member who is least able to keep up with things — make sure she or he is taking it in).

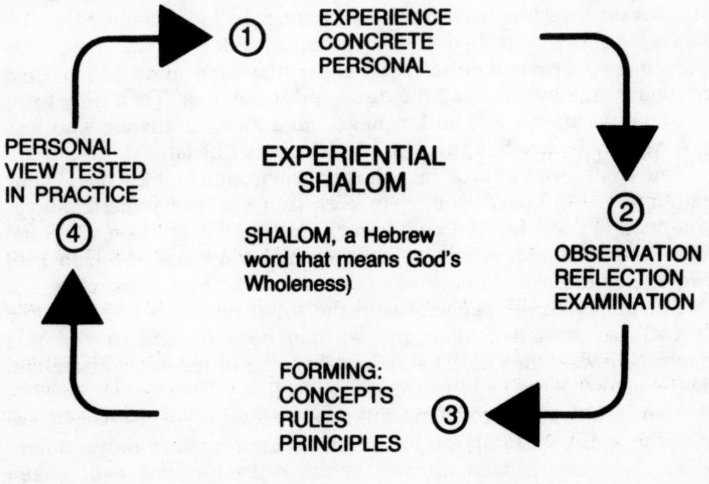

This model means:
1. We have an activity that creates feelings and a concrete experience.
2. We can then look back at it and examine what has happened (it's easier to examine something that has *just* happened rather than last year! or last week!).
3. From this 'Reflection' we can perhaps change our ideas. From this examination we can understand better and re-look at the 'rules' we make about life.
4. After the group has finished today — we can then put into practice the things we have decided to do.

First Half
Buzz Feelings

Introduce this item by asking the group members to listen to reading 1 below in silence and take in the feelings. Use a good reader because the main reason for this item is to make the illustration 'live'!

Reading 1

Youth to youth worker

It was an ordinary evening at the club, but it was obvious that trouble was brewing. I turned round from chatting to a group of kids to see what seemed to be a mass of bodies involved in something that looked horrible. Someone was picking up pool balls and hurling them violently towards a boy who was already being kicked and punched by four or five others.

A fight had started in the club and I had known it was coming. The atmosphere had been tense all evening. Included among the 200 teenagers present we had a large group of older teenage boys who were out to prove themselves. They stood in a large group in a dominant area overlooking the disco and social area. Their only form of communication was foul language and a kick for anyone who was passing. There was bound to be trouble sooner or later.

You can't just 'police' in a hostile environment like this. Your emotions are stretched, you try to keep your eyes everywhere and yet you need to *seem* relaxed and active. This was my position when the fight broke out. An Asian-looking boy had come into the club with two white girls. Asians normally never enter the Mayflower club, but due to the extensive publicity with the smart new club opening, one or two had started coming and we had been pleased to welcome them. Normally they didn't stay long because of the racist abuse and harassment that we were unable to control.

Alan, Doug and Geoff (my full-time colleagues) and myself were into the mêlée instantly and it stopped briefly before more violent kicks and punches were thrown at the badly bleeding and shaken visitor. He was taken down to my office by Doug while the other workers tried to deal with the violent and bitter racist atmosphere. 'We were only pulling others off him,' said the four regular club members, grinning sickly. We had got to know these boys over the previous five years, loved them, prayed for them and yet they were still violent, aggressive teenagers.

In the office I tried desperately to relate to a young man who was highly agitated, insulted, bitter, humiliated and covered in blood. Doug was bandaging him, for he was bleeding badly from a head wound caused by a pool ball. I tried to apologise, explain, express our hurt, before he was driven away to hospital in a quickly borrowed minibus. The bitter racist atmosphere was still evident in the club. There were laughs from both sexes. 'Did you see him bleed? His blood was black!' 'The next best thing to a dead dog is a dead Paki!' It is impossible to express the immensity of hurt and hate evident that evening.

During his journey to the hospital Doug found out that the young man's nationality was South American! It didn't matter to the attackers — he *looked* like a Paki! The club continued but we knew quite well that we would have to stand with this young visitor against our members. Justice meant our standing against any racist attack and this justice was instantly offered to the visitor.

The next day was even worse. There were two probation officers in my office when the four boys concerned with the attack came round, having heard that the police were after them, and realising our obvious involvement as witnesses. Threats were directed at me with such ferocity that it shook me to the core. Inside I was shaking. I am certain that if the probation officers hadn't been there the attack would have been physical, and I felt protected by their presence. 'We are coming to smash the place up Sunday,' were their parting words.

All this resulted in some horrible days. The members concerned were known to be going through a very violent time of their lives. It affected me deeply. I was unable to sleep for two nights; I was afraid to walk the streets; I was scared for our kids. Joan, my wife, was waking up in the middle of the night and retching in the toilet. The tension for my family was so great — yet it was second-hand tension, all being passed on from me.

The police were involved, not only in searching for the attackers, but we also had to bring plain clothes police into the club for protection. In the East End culture you can do no worse than 'grass' on someone. That was what we were seen to be doing — and for a 'Paki' too. But we believed in justice — God's justice.

The tension lasted some weeks because after arrest the boys were released on bail pending their trial, which would be months later.

Later the same week I was in the disco crowded with lots of young teenagers enjoying themselves when Joan, one of our youth workers,

pushed through to me. 'Pip, Jon is in and he's got a knife . . .' She took the office key to phone the 'Old Bill' (police) and I sat on the window ledge in the disco, hiding in our own club as teenagers danced around me. Five years of work with teenagers in East London and I needed to hide out of the way. I felt sick. At the same time, one of my experienced, professionally-trained colleagues was also hiding, sitting on the floor of the office, shaking.
Extract taken from: *Gutter Feelings* by Pip Wilson (Marshalls, 1985) £1.95.

(*a*) On conclusion the participants are asked to note their feelings. Pick one word that describes your feelings.
Leader Notes: this is YOUR Group — you know it better than anyone! But be extra aware! Be extra observant by looking at every member and checking that no one feels left out. Always thank anyone who makes a contribution. Never be negative to *any* response, because it affects the whole group. In this exercise encourage lots of members to share one or two words that describe their feelings on hearing the reading. Some will start to give their opinions. Interrupt! Thank them but ask again for FEELINGS not thoughts.
Note the words on a large piece of paper on the wall. Affirm, encourage and then move on to (*b*).

(*b*) Members are asked to share in groups of threes their *own* experience of violence — received/observed or even created themselves.

Role Play

Leader Notes: don't call it role play *if* you feel it will inhibit the group.

This will give participants authentic feelings of being brought up in a violent/emotionally charged family. Read this part several times and become familiar with it. Visualise it happening with your group and how it can function in your building. It is a very powerful tool. It has been used many times and is well worth the effort.

1. Split everyone into 'threes'. If there is an extra one or two create a couple of 'fours' rather than only 'twos'.
   Don't join a group yourself but *everyone* else needs to participate.
2. Get them to label themselves A, B, C etc.
3. Tell them that this is a game which lasts only a minute and will be very useful (but don't, at this stage, give away what the activity will be).
4. Explain that 'A' is to be an *observer* and he/she is to watch and listen intently and then report back.
5. *Explain* 'B' is a parent of a child 'C' of approximately 8–9 years old.
6. Then send all 'C's out of the room.

7. Brief the parents 'B' saying your child will shortly come in and treat them normally as a parent should.
8. Brief 'C's outside the room and ask them to play the part seriously as it will only last for one minute.

THE FIRST PHASE

9. Then send in the 'children' quickly and allow the role play to happen for one minute or so.
   Expect some messing about and nervous laughter and a whole range of extroverts and embarrassed participants.
10. Then ask the observer what happened, and get them to feedback quickly.

THE SECOND PHASE

11. Choose new observer, parent and child. The same role play is repeated: do it a total of three times.
12. The second time out, *emphasise* more and more the need not to laugh and mess about as it takes away from the 'experience'. Brief the parent like this . . .
    'When your child comes in from school give her/him 15 seconds or so of attention and affection. Then for remainder of time completely ignore or become distracted by watching TV, or reading or getting dinner ready etc. Do this whatever happens with the child.' Emphasise the need to play the role seriously.
13. *Brief to the child*
    'You are an 8/9 year old coming home from school with some good news: top of class, picked for football team or school holiday . . . use own ideas. Be very enthusiastic but real, not silly. Try and get into the feelings of a delighted child.'
14. On debriefing, following the role play, ask the observers but follow it by asking for *feeling* words from the 'children'.

THE THIRD PHASE

This is the final and the most powerful phase.

15. *Brief to the parent*
    'When your child has gone to school this morning you enter her/his bedroom and it is a terrible, worse than ever, condition of untidiness. For weeks now your child has been promising to tidy up the room and this is the last straw. Get into the frame of mind to really sort out the problem "once and for all" when the child comes home from school.'
16. *Brief for child*
    'On your way home from school, you have seen something that upsets you. An accident or similar event. Get into the feelings of this. When you enter the room you really want to tell your parent all about it.
    Allow for seconds for the 'child' to choose their particular upsetting incident and get into the 'role'.

17. Expect some emotion in this one. Tears, bad feeling, sad faces and extreme feelings.
When you debrief at the end of this one keep people quiet because if they chat and laugh they will lose their 'feelings' which is what we wish to learn from.

Particularly at this stage collect the feeling words from both 'children' and 'parents' leaving observers to come in at the end.
The feelings will be real, not *acting*.
After people have explained their feelings make the following points.
(i) These feelings were structured for learning (point to the Experiential Shalom chart).
(ii) These feelings were created in a one minute role play, yet they are very *real*.
(iii) You (the Leader) accept responsibility for the feelings created because you led them into it. Explain that you *planned* that the two agendas collided. The parent had an agenda. The child had an agenda. It is so often the case in real life.

Special note

It is important at the end of any emotionally charged role play to allow all participants a period of time to *de-role*. This can be best done by giving each group of three, time to chat these individual feelings through.
De-roling is different to de-briefing.
De-briefing is part of the package of learning from the role play.
De roling is actually leaving the role behind and affirming 'self'– affirming reality.
For example '*I am* Pip Wilson, I have a wife Joan, daughters Ann and Joy – I have been through the learning experience. I am *not* . . . (whatever role has ben played) I am . . . etc.'
If you plan to have tea or coffee during the evening the best time is now.

Second Half

Supply each member with paper and pencil and have them record 'feeling words' during the following readings (they have had some recent practice at this and should be good by now!).
Alternative — supply members with the 'Feeling Faces' sheet (see page 138).

Two Readings

Members are asked to record feeling words to the following two readings.
An introduction explains that these are extreme examples of violence.

Reading 2 These readings are extreme examples of violence. Please write feelings as they are read.
The Guardian 15/2/86
'A West German film-maker yesterday presented unique film footage taken after the liberation of Auschwitz which had been kept in the archives of a Soviet cameraman for 40 years. It is the only record of the camp after its liberation on January 22, 1945. The hour-long film shows pictures of emaciated survivors, rotting corpses, mass graves, and camp installations. Long passages of the film are devoted to the work of Soviet doctors examining child victims of medical experiments and torture, gathered by the Russians as evidence for the prosecution at the Nuremberg war crimes trials. The silent footage also has stark images of the 6,000 Auschwitz survivors, and the perverse meticulousness of the Nazi death machine.
Russian soldiers are seen, holding up babies' clothes stripped by the Nazis from their victims, and discovering 43,000 bags of shaven hair which the Nazis recycled for socks and thread.
The Russians walk past piled-up clothing, shoes, shaving brushes, spectacles, jewellery and gold teeth and fillings which the Nazis melted into 12 kilogrammes of gold a day.
The Russians documented 350,000 men's suits, 840,000 women's dresses and 16 million pairs of shoes found in the camp.'

Leader Notes Get some feedback from the group: – feelings; any other comments.
Note any comments that suggested that the group members expected physical violence between individuals or teenage gangs rather than historical mass murder.
Encourage a little reflection on the different forms of violence.

Reading 3
The Guardian, February '86
'One night, five youths were assaulted when a van load of adults jumped out and "kicked and punched" the youths. "Two of them needed hospital treatment." '
Twenty-four adults knew about the crime but the eight concerned could not be traced.
It was a cover-up. The youths were assaulted by uniformed police officers on duty in the Holloway Road, North London. All twenty-four were interviewed but none confessed. The police magazine 'Police Review' in an article headed '*A Conspiracy of Bastards*' said 'Why was there not one officer with the guts to denounce the uniformed criminals?'
Note for leader: at the time of writing a number of officers have now been arrested and charged and the case has yet to come to court.

Discuss political violence, state violence, alongside any personal violence that may be currently in the news locally or nationwide. Encourage the young people to ask questions *beyond* the TV/newspapers versions.

Bible Study

This part looks at the Bible and faces us with the question of 'What attitude does the Bible demonstrate in these passages?' Choose one or more of these passages — whichever is most relevant to the group. Or, distribute them all among small groups of 5–8 participants with the question 'What can we learn from this Bible passage?'

Jesus and Violence

1. *Luke 4:5–8*. Jesus rejected physical force; when Satan tempted him with all the political and military power in the World.
2. *John 8:1–11*. Jesus disapproved of punishing an adulteress by violence.
3. *Matthew 26:47–56*. Although powerful Jesus rejected force.
4. *Matthew 5:39–43*. What should our response to violence be?
5. *Luke 23:32–34*. Jesus died by an act of violence, 'crucifixion', but he said 'Father forgive'.

'The Kingdom is not where power rules and people compete, but where Love rules.'

Conclusion

Point again to the Experiential model. Ask young people to answer in small groups (3–4).

Question 1 'In what way have my attitudes changed towards violence?'

Question 2 'Am I willing to be different than my friends, my family, this group, the Leader, because of any new or slightly different attitudes?'

Affirm and encourage the participants to think beyond the news headlines and thank *them* for making the session so worthwhile.

Resource 1

Violence In The Family

'It is safer to be on the streets after dark with a stranger than at home with one's family.'

4,600 children are physically abused each year. Of these, 700 will die and 400 will be left with permanent brain damage. Approximately half of the murders are followed by suicide or attempted suicide.

Extreme violence and death usually involve the father or male custodian of the child, rather than the mother.

Doctor Peter Scott studied 29 men charged with killing a child under 5 years old. Two thirds were not married to their partners, and half were not the father of the victim. 20 of the 29 were considered to have significant personality disorders.

Doctor Selwyn Smith has studied the cases of 134 battered babies, their 125 mothers and 89 of their fathers. 15 per cent of the babies died and 15 per cent received permanent damage. One third of the mothers were unmarried and three quarters had conceived pre-maritally. The mothers were nearly four years below the national average age at the birth of the first child. Most of the mothers were considered to be emotionally immature and dependent. Two thirds of the fathers had a personality disorder and one third a criminal record.

Doctor John Gayford studied 100 battered wives and published the following statistics. 44 per cent of the 'husbands' involved were immigrants, 21 per cent from Ireland and 13 per cent from the West Indies. 44 per cent of the 'wives' received lacerated wounds, 9 per cent were knocked unconscious, 2 per cent had retinal damage and 2 per cent experienced post-traumatic epilepsy.

Thirty-four of the women had attempted suicide, ten more than once. Thirty-seven of the women admitted that they in turn discharged their frustration in violence towards the children. Twenty-three of the women and fifty-one of the men had been exposed to family violence in childhood. Fifty-one of the men had been in prison or borstal, thirty-three for violent offences, and twenty-nine were unemployed. Gambling was a problem in twenty-five of the families.

The marriage or cohabitation was often precipitated and related to a desire to leave home, commencing in fifty-eight cases without preliminary courtship. Eighty-six women had regular sexual intercourse without contraception before marriage, at which stage sixty were pregnant. All but nineteen had separated at least once, and twenty-five had been battered by their present partner before marriage or cohabitation.

Birch and Chess, in *Behavioural individuality in early childhood*, note that those women who do break with their violent husbands, a disturbing number enter into another relationship more violent than the first.

Resource 2

Questions on Violence

LOVE: 'It always protects, always trusts, always hopes, always perseveres.' 1 Corinthians 13

The opposite of *Agape* (love) is apathy.

'And He will be called Prince of *Peace*'. *Shalom*: wholeness, well-being.

We live in a violent world. Few people will condone violence for the sake of violence, but the Chrstian is called to consider the matter further.

Is all violence evil?
Should Christians be pacifists?
Is there such a thing as 'righteous violence'?
What constitutes violence? attitudes? thoughts? or only actions?
What is pacifism? Can it be fighting for peace?
How far does the use of violence combat violence and how much further it?

Some biblical considerations

1 Samuel 15:18.	An example of the violence done for the furtherance of Israel. How does this apply to the use of violence for a good cause? Does it?
Amos 2:7; 5:24	The concern of the prophet for action on behalf of the needy, the poor, the orphan, the widow. What is the worth of faith without action?
Matthew 21:12 Mark 11:12 Luke 19:45 John 2:12	How can righteous anger become righteous action? Is this an example of Jesus being violent?
Ephesians 4:26	What is the relation between anger and violence? How far should we allow our anger to go? Should we put a limit on our actions of violence?
Ephesians 6:5	Should we act at all? Should we just accept the situation? Do we accept the situation for ourselves and only act for others? Is this verse relevant to the consideration of violence?
Matthew 5:38ff.	What does Jesus say? How do we apply this? How do we relate this to the need for action? We must be concerned for love, justice and protection. How can we love both parties?

Psalm 139	This Psalm talks about the value and importance of each person. This applies to those who do the violence as well as those who are the 'receivers' doesn't it? Are we any more in the right if we use violence against them? On the other hand, how can we non-violently stop their violence?

Resource 3

Book List

Christ and Violence Ronald Sider (Lion, 1979).

An Introduction to Non-Violence Training (Peace News Collective, 1982).

The Politics of Love — The New Testament and Non-Violent Revolution J. Ferguson (J. Clarke & Co, 1973).

'Hooligan' — A history of respectable fears G. Pearson.

Violence Jacques Ellul (Eerdmans, Seabury, 1969).

Violence — edited by Norman Tutt (Department of Health & Social Security, 1976).

Victory Over Violence M. Hengel.

It is Not Lawful for Me to Fight J. M. Hornus.

The Peaceable Kingdom S. Hauerwas (University of Notre Dame Press, 1983).

The Ethics of War Paskins and Dockerill.

Moral Problems Narvesson.

Murder Mystery

Numbers

Total numbers a maximum of 20–24. 6–10 participating and the remainder as observers

Equipment

22 clue cards typed (as per instructions).
Paper or pencil for everyone.

Details

Aim: to solve a problem and learn about life.
The task: Find out
The Murderer
The Weapon
The Time
The Place
The Motive

Leader's instructions
The Method

1. Type all the clues on separate cards. (Don't type the numbers.)
2. Sit group members on the floor in a circle.
3. Leave 3 or more outside the circle as observers.
4. Shuffle the cards and distribute them all evenly amongst group.
5. The clues can only be communicated verbally and NOT shown to other members or swopped around.
6. Give the group 10 minutes to accomplish the task.
7. Call out when 5 minutes is left and so on every minute. This puts pressure on participants and increases the value of the game.
8. If the task isn't complete after 10 minutes allow extra time under pressure until the task is finished.

At the end give out correct answer (See Appendix Four)

Aim. This is a puzzle 'who dunnit' game and is great to observe the group in action. The *observers* are asked to:
1. Forget the mystery and the task. Their role is observing all verbal and non-verbal communication.
2. Some things to watch out for:

Who talks first
Who looks at who
Who is the quietest
Who makes suggestions
Who cracks jokes
Who is ignored
Who is opting out
Who puts pressure on group
Who is hurtful or insensitive
Who moves bodily closer to the group
Who moves bodily away from group
Were the resources shared?
Was the group co-operative?
How were the decision made?
What problems were there?
Was the decision unanimous?

Clues: to be typed on individual cards

1. Steve Butler was found dead. When he was discovered he had a bullet wound in his thigh and a knife wound in his chest.
2. Charles Longeneker shot an intruder in his flat at 2.00 a.m.
3. Charles Longeneker's garage business had been made bankrupt following Steve Butler's wheeling and dealing.
4. The Police were given information by the lift operator, that he last saw Mr Butler at 2.15 a.m.
5. Charles Longeneker's gun matched the bullet taken from Steve Butler's thigh.
6. Mr Longeneker's gun had only fired one bullet.
7. The lift operator said that Mr Butler wasn't badly hurt.
8. In the basement a knife was found. It had been wiped clean of all fingerprints.
9. Mrs Wilson had been waiting in the foyer for her husband to finish work.
10. At 2.30 a.m. the lift operator went off duty.
11. The dead body of Steve Butler was found near the dustbin area.
12. Steve Butler's body was found at 3.05 a.m.
13. The body was examined and had been dead for one hour before it was found.
14. Steve Butler was not seen to leave by Mrs Wilson while she waited in the foyer.
15. Bloodstains of the same type as Steve Butler were found in the basement garage.
16. Mr Longeneker couldn't be located by police after the murder.
17. Bloodstains found outside Mr Longeneker's flat corresponded with Mr Butler's blood type.

18. Bloodstains were found in the lift.
19. Regular visits had been made to Mr Butler's flat by Mrs Wilson.
20. Mrs Wilson's husband had been jealous of their friendship.
21. At the end of normal working hours Mrs. Wilson's husband did not appear. He didn't arrive by 2 30 a.m. so she returned home and he arrived later.
22. Mrs Wilson could not find her car or her husband in the basement garage of the block of flats where he worked.

See answer in Appendix Four on p. 184.

Discussion

There may well be a period at the end of the game when the total topic of conversation is 'the murder' mystery. Once the members have satisfied themselves as to their success or failure leave that topic and quickly get onto the real purpose of the game — the learning.

Suggested ways of handling the learning

1. Ask the participants to share their feelings at the end of the game or during the game.
2. Ask the observers to share their observations: what they *heard* and *saw*, body language, e.g. contact, touch, people moving physically into or out of the group, loud talkers, overtalkers, questioners, encouragers, disrupters, blockers, comedians, leaders.
3. Ask the group participants what they have learned of their own behaviour in this group. Is it typical of their normal response to a group at work, in church, in their club or fellowship?
4. *General Discussion Question*. How can we 'love' people with our eyes body language, sensitivity, leadership?

Bible readings/discussion

1. John 13:35. I give you a new commandment: love one another. As I have loved you so you must love one another. If you have love for one another then everyone will know that you are my disciples.

Discussion question

How can we communicate the good news of Jesus non-verbally?

2. Luke 15:11. The Prodigal Son.

Look at these people.

The Prodigal Son, the Father, the Older Brother.

Listen and discuss their non-verbal communication, both positive and negative.

Translate their positive actions into the lives of the individual group members.

Make one decision now which will change your attitudes and behaviour.

The Cross of Ashes

Numbers

Large or small

Equipment

Self standing wooden cross (see details).
One sheet of A4 paper.

Details

Preamble. This is a visual aid that can be used in many different situations. In youth clubs, talks, house parties etc. This is the basic explanation but please adapt and introduce it to make it relevant to the particular context you are in.

Cross Visual Aid

1. Make a self-standing cross approximately two feet high.
2. Half knock a 2″ nail in centre of cross.
3. Pass a piece of A4 white duplicating paper around the group to *every* member. (Use duplicating paper; the thinner types don't work as well.) Get everyone to sign their own name (or nickname if they prefer).
4. This can be done with few words, many or even no words.
   - i. Introduce the paper as being personal to everyone present. We all have our name on (add your own!).
   - ii. When Jesus went to the cross(punch the paper over the nail as illustrated) he went to the cross for *you* — and for all of us.
   - iii. He took with him *all* our wrongs, *everything* that separates us from God, from each other, from our communities, from the wholeness of life.
   - iv. He died for us (strike a match and dramatically light both bottom corners of paper and, in silence, let it burn into a blackened shrivelled and fragile disfigurement).
   - v. It cost Jesus pain, hurt and total humility as he was crucified as a criminal.
   - vi. He died this horrible death and yet even though he has gone (take from the cross 'the remains', gently in both hands, walking out into the audience crush into dust and scatter on the floor) . . . even though he has gone — disappeared —

he has returned — in fact he still lives — He *lives* — and is available to make a relationship with.

vii. By that one act he makes possible: new relationships; exciting living; aim and purpose; world peace; health and hope. *His* response to our needs for freedom and liberation requires a response from you which will reach beyond a personal faith; to family; friends; your community; politics and nations and a world at war.

5. Be economical with words. Use silences and allow people to interpret and apply the visual aid to their own lives.
6. Many Bible verses can be used. This one opens up the possibility of wholeness for our lives, our family, our community, nation and beyond into world issues.
   '. . . *Shalom* through Jesus . . .' has implications beyond our simple meaning of 'Peace'. It relates to wholeness in every sector of society. Every breath — every issue. Jesus died for our wholeness.

The Bible (TEV)
Colossians Chapter 1 Verse 20.
Through the Son then, God decided to bring the whole universe back to himself. God made *SHALOM* through his Son's death on the cross and so brought back to himself all things both on earth and in heaven.

Appendix One

Games Leader Preparation Sheet

Need to lead a games session?

GUT GAMES PREPARATION SHEET

Ask these questions to yourself or ....

Key Contact

NOTES

Date ....
Day..
Arrival Time ....
Start Time ....
Finish ime ....

Size of Hall (Venue)..
Ceiling High/Low ....
Stage Fixed ....
Portable ....
Height ....
Width ....
Depth ....
Power points & situation ....
Lighting ....
Sound System ....
Catering Facilities ....

Ages ....
Numbers ....
Male ....
Female ....
Social Background ....
Normal Social Interests ....
One Group ....
Cohesive ....
Individuals of Note ....
Christian Commitment ....
Local Tension ....
Local Issues/Concerns ....
Recent Programme ....
Attitude to Messy Games ....
Attitude to Christian Games ....
Expectations of Participants ....
Expectation of Organisers ....

Appendix Two

Gut Game Questions

These are a whole collection of questions for you to use to create discussion, self revelation, level 5 sharing and ice-breaking, etc.
Use as you wish when you wish.
Add to the list, collect your own.
Use current questions by looking at the daily newspapers, TV News, TV Soaps etc.

Please Note
Just *one* of these questions used *well* could be used for a whole evening's group session. In fact, to open up a topic and not to give it sufficient time could be a negative experience.

Gut Games — Ideas for Questions

What's your favourite colour?
What colour are you (not skin colour, but the colour that describes you personally)?
What colour is God?
What animal would be most like your personality?
What part of your life is rich?
What part of your life is poor?
When did you become an adult?
What is your favourite scar?
What body part would you swop?
What makes you angry?
Who was the source of warmth when you were five years old?
When did God first become a source of warmth (if ever)?
Have you ever been shoplifting?
What is your favourite hobby?
What is your favourite time of the day?
What is your favourite place in your home?
What is your favourite season of the year?
When did you last cry?
Do you like your name?
Who would you like to be stuck in a lift with?
Who cleans your toilet?
What is highest on your emotional agenda?
What makes you sad?

What sort of car are you? (What most fits your personality?)
What sort of car is God?
At what time of the day do you most think, reflect?
What has been your biggest failure?
Describe an ambition.
What is your favourite TV programme?
Where would you like to be now?
What new name would you choose?
Where in the world would you like to go on holiday?
Who is an authority figure in your life?
Describe a young person who you know.
What task have you most on your mind?
Which members of the opposite sex come quickly to mind?
When did you stop being a child?
When you get in the bath which bit do you wash first?
What would you do with nuclear weapons?
Would you rather be the Prime Minister or his/her bodyguard?
Do you like kissing?
Who is the best hugger in your life?
What do you do with your toe nails when they have been cut?
In which way are you blind?
What present would you like to receive?
What is your favourite animal?
What present would you like to give?
What is your favourite book?
What is your favourite film/video?
Who understands you best?
What is your wish for yourself?
What is your wish for your group?
What is your wish for your community?
What is your wish for your country?
What is your wish for your polititians?
What is your wish for your world?
Which injustice first comes to mind?
What animal is most like you?
With which person do you feel most uncomfortable?
Describe yourself without mentioning anything you *do*.
Which group do you belong to more than any other?
Tell one lie about one of your values.
Describe a most beautiful thing.
What makes you most stressful?
Can you remember, and describe it, the last time you held the hand of a very young baby?
What do you have in your possession now that you would give to someone in need?
Think of a 'church' and describe your feelings.

What do you think was the greatest point in history?
What would you like to smash?
How important is money to you?
If you knew you couldn't fail what would you do?
What do you think about nudity?
What do you think about inter-racial dates and marriage?
What parable in the Bible do you remember?
What makes you sad?
What concerns you most about your health?
What are you impressed by in the life of Jesus?
Who is the warmest person in your life?
Who has most helped you to understand God?
What should you be arrested for?
Which do you think is the worst crime that can be committed?
What character of God means most to you?
What is the most serious lie you have told?
What is the big question you have for God to answer?
Have you cheated in exams?
What does faith mean to you?
What do you think about the value of women in society?
What do you feel about swearing?
Did/do you enjoy school?
Describe a person in your life who is the most real/whole person.
What do you think about punishment?
What has been the greatest discovery?
Can you remember being punished as a child?
When do you feel alone the most?
When do you feel most alive?
Who would you like to be attracted to you?
Would you take an illegal drug?
Name one association/organisation that you disapprove of.
What person in history would you like to have been?
Describe your normal day in one minute.
Describe your perfect day in one minute.
When you were five years old in what way was your home heated?
When you were five years old which person was the source of warmth?
Can you remember when God first became a source of warmth?
What is not of value but valuable to you?

Appendix Three

A Reaction Sheet

This is my favourite reaction sheet that I invented and have used over many years.
Ideal Use: after every game session, training course, meeting etc.

REACTION SHEET NAME . . . .

Circle one answer for each question

1. How helpful was the session?

*	*	*	*	*	*	*	*
very poor	poor	mediocre	fair	good	very good	excellent	best ever

---

2. To what extent did it deal with your real interests/needs?

*	*	*	*	*	*
not at all	a bit	some		very much	right on

---

3. What was the main strength?

....

....

....

---

4. What was the main weakness?

....

....

....

Appendix Four

Answer to Murder Mystery p. 174

Mr Longeneker had shot Mr Butler in the thigh. As Mr Butler went into the lift he was killed by Mr Wilson (the lift operator) with a knife at 2.05 because he was jealous.

Alphabetical Index

Category Index

Sources/Ideas

Recommended Books for the Group Leader/Worker	*Publisher*
Serendipity Series	SU
Gamesters' Handbook	Hutchinson
Over 300 games for all occasions	SU
Non Competitive Games	Bethany House, U.S.A.

IS IT
FINISHED
?
I am